D0555705

ARCHIVES OF THE HEATHENS VOL. I

ARCHIVES OF THE HEATHENS VOL. I

TALES OF A SECRET SOCIETY ON THE RMS MAURETANIA 1908 TO 1914

DR. B. S. JONES

Copyright © 2016 by Dr. B. S. Jones.

Library of Congress Control Number:		2016904511
ISBN:	Hardcover	978-1-5144-7686-4
	Softcover	978-1-5144-7685-7
	eBook	978-1-5144-7684-0

All rights reserved. No part of this book may be reproduced or transmitted in any form or by any means, electronic or mechanical, including photocopying, recording, or by any information storage and retrieval system, without permission in writing from the copyright owner.

Any people depicted in stock imagery provided by Thinkstock are models, and such images are being used for illustrative purposes only.
Certain stock imagery © Thinkstock.

Print information available on the last page.

Rev. date: 04/26/2016

To order additional copies of this book, contact:
Xlibris
1-888-795-4274
www.Xlibris.com
Orders@Xlibris.com
721297

"O God! Put back Thy universe and
give me yesterday"

Henry Arthur Jones

PREFACE

BORED, DAMAGED, AND having too much free time led me to become a collector of first edition books. Since childhood I have always had a love for reading, devouring science fiction. As with most readers, other concerns stole time from that pursuit. Perusing eBay one night, I viewed an auction of books from the decommissioning of the RMS *Mauretania* in 1935 that another collector had found in a box long forgotten.

The first two, of which I was outbid, were first editions, specially bound in leather for the ship's library. A week later the untitled binder, upon which this book is based, was listed. This contained several signatures of famous people, the seller focusing on the value of the autographs. The book markedly interested me in that strange sense you never wholly grasp. I bid with five seconds to go in an auction, a classic "sniper." The price was around a hundred dollars and had generated very few bids. I typed in a "nuke 'em" number, just in case someone really wanted the item. One more buyer had the same idea and doubled the current price, but my "nuke number" was considerably beyond reason and the other bidders doubling. I felt compelled to buy it.

The book arrived; tattered, spine exposed to bare fibers, and pancaked from years of being crushed by heavier books. I verified the valuable signatures and briefly inspected the miscellaneous contents—signed menus, personal photos, a half-dozen typed pages, cards, —and noticed the title on the cover, *Archives of the Heathens.* I put the book in a drawer. My inspired enthusiasm was cast aside.

Six months later, curiosity returned, and I wondered: Who were the 169 people that had signed the book? Who were these Heathens? A five-year quest began. The names had to be deciphered and identified, not an easy task, most were unfamiliar, and numerous others penned erratically. Hours of frustration mingled with increasing success until only a handful remained anonymous. Soon I realized this was a unique document, which revealed an extraordinary tale of an unlikely union of travelers.

The ensuing research uncovered that many of these people had been very well-known personages in the first quarter of the last century, some with fascinating stories. With ghostly encouragement, I put fingertips to keyboard. Inevitably, I awakened the forsaken Heathen family, finding myself in appropriate company. Oddly, they referred to each other as "brother" & "sister", something I had done for years on the streets of Cleveland, Ohio during a period of marital readjustment. Refreshingly, all contained herein is true and accurate to the best of my limited abilities, although a spoonful of fiction was added to facilitate the story. The discerning historian may find previously unknown facts about members of the secret society.

Regrettably, families I was able to contact for pictures of their relatives from that era were less than forthcoming, a small number in England responded generously. ELLinSpain assisted me at the beginning of this venture by kindly researching passenger lists on Ancestry.com. If the stars guide you to the website listed herein you can view the accumulated artifacts, pictures, and other miscellanies associated with the Heathens I have posted. The interactive site is RmsMauretaniaHeathenArchive.org or you can find the Heathens on *Facebook* at Archive of the Heathens, RMS Mauretania.

Ah! Could we but fathom the mighty deep
And count up the treasures there
Or tell of the noble spirits gone
To the home so lone and drear;
Tis when we can feel as the sailor feels
When his lonely watch he keeps,
And hears 'midst the howling and raging storm
The voice of the mighty deep,
The voice of the mighty deep
Sadly telling the tale of brave hearts that sleep
Ah! Never to rise again.

—Arthur E. Harrison

IN THE UNLIKELY event hell should freeze over, do not kill an albatross. It has been whispered among weathered mariners that under favorable circumstances, you may, on a very special occasion, be able to entice the essence of a vanished seafaring soul from the fabled seabird. I am dead longer than most of you have been alive, and increasingly so. My departure was a chronic occurrence of predictable nature, the mind yielded to a most persistent body. A few surviving family and ambulatory friends attended a modest service, a year before the Second World War came to an end. When blessed to outlive most of your peers, one is fortunate to have anyone beyond the resurrection-man.

Prior to exhausting my vitality, I could be found sailing the "Sea of Atlas," on a sizeable ship, attending to the needs of passengers and crew. For six years I was entrusted the supplementary task of ministering a wayward troupe of very notable, extremely jovial, and mostly incorrigible individuals. Without provocation, a mystifying sorcery has briefly reclaimed my halcyon spirit. I imagine a single purpose for this: our tales must be told, and with urgency. The tide is favorable. Cast away the ropes holding your mind in the present, and meet me at the landing stage at Liverpool. Today is 15 September 1908. Do not dawdle, it is not as far as you imagine.

My name is B. Sydney Jones, chief surgeon of the RMS *Mauretania*, and I cordially receive you aboard the newest ship in the Cunard fleet. I am most assured my name will not revive any memory, nor should it, but with further reading, I will abet your journey from uncharted to abreast. Upon graduation from medical college, I found myself restless on *terra firma* and sought adventure on *mare incognita*, something more buoyant beckoned. Furthermore, I was determined to be free of my father's long shadow. Becoming a Cunard surgeon seemed perfectly natural for my now so precious youthful exuberance. Imaginably, it was the reflection of the dashing, uniformed gentleman I saw in my mental looking glass. More likely, it was how distinguished I would look to the ladies. Recently promoted from surgeon on the RMS *Lucania*, I perceived my new position as a great responsibility, but alas, along came those amiable, peripatetic bon vivants. Abiding is my obligation.

My remaining efforts shall be to salvage one's most precious possessions: memories. All are true to the best of my remembrances. Pardon me for a bit. The sudden return has left me muddled. I had never envisioned the possibility of being reinvigorated in mind and deed, so bear with me. I remain bewildered as to how the sacred book of our exploits found its scribbles in the twenty-first century, one hundred years after being so irreverently marooned. However improbable, I shall not be further troubled. I am sardined with an untold narrative. Stories must be told to be remembered.

> The twentieth century was born without a memory
> It's so busy with today's achievements and
> Tomorrow's projects that no one has time
> To remember yesterday's exploits.
>
> —Herbert Kaufman,
> *The Winning Fight*, 1911

History is scarred by wars. The never-ending cycles of destruction and creation must be demanding overlords, for history imitates men. With the advent of the new century, Britain had fresh memories of the Second Boer War. America was only ten years removed from the Spanish-American War. Article 25 of the Treaty of Berlin was causing increasing resentment and anger in a piddling Balkan country called

Serbia. I remember the Second Boer War. While serving on the SS *Catalonia,* the ship was impolitely removed from its routine Boston to Liverpool passenger route. For that unpleasant assignment, she was converted into a prison ship for captured Dutch farmers off the coast of what would become South Africa. While anchored two miles from shore in Simon's Bay, those pesky farmers proved quite meddlesome with repeated attempts at escape into the water, most being recaptured.

Shanghaied from my place of serenity a mere moment ago, there is an ongoing debate. Fellow doctor Sigmund Freud has a most outlandish opinion on the causation of the man's worldly conflicts. His theory pertains to glandula mammaria, uteri, unresolved sexual issues, and man's subconscious mind. Dr. Jones has no sentiments on the controversy, but his thoughts revert toward that old conundrum about a chicken and an egg. I am equally unsettled resolving whether or not a canary can hatch an ostrich egg and why my favorite bird is the JubJub, not a parrot. Freud did depict the human mind as an iceberg, which, after encountering several from close range, I found no such similarities.

Aeroplanes and their daring pilots excited the people. Wireless messages made communication over great oceans nearly instantaneous. Ransom Olds, a young automobile maker, had recently installed the first assembly line in Detroit to mass produce the Curved Dash Oldsmobile. Nevertheless, the modern, swift, streamlined steamships garnered the greatest attention of my generation. How could the fair Duchess of Roxburghe, Anne Innes-Ker, have anticipated when she christened our majestic hull, that she was bestowing upon the great liner such esteem and endurance.

Allow a ration of leniency for my pride. I shall use the varnish sparingly. Ships during my era were floating palatial palaces. The *Mauretania* was constructed for the supreme comfort of the leisurely traveler or seasoned businessman, and it displayed sumptuously. Only superior materials in the hands of prodigious craftsmen adorned the interiors and premier foods and liquors were provided. Everything was truly first-rate.

Entertainments of varied sorts were available, shuffleboard being fashonable, but most found the deck chair conspicuously sensible. Musical performances are provided by the best bands, and their leaders were outstanding. Each crossing was hallmarked with a Seamen's Charity Concert to raise money for the sailor's relief fund. We were fortunate to have had the famous Wallace Hartley for five years, but he left for the *Titanic* when he was "persuaded" to take that position. The ship was alive with music from afternoon long into the eventide. Gambling was nightly in the richly lacquered walnut-paneled smoking room.

In contrast, it was very much a "velvet rope" ship—the separation of classes was strictly enforced. Being a doctor, I found the practice disconcerting. Sickness has no monetary barriers. Despite economic distinctions, our ship's constantly being booked was testimony to the services we offered. Steady as she goes, my ghost is trying to secure passage for you on a ship that, for the time being, can only navigate the troughs and crests within my mind.

Mauretania was an ancient Roman province in Northwest Africa; you are more familiar with it as Morocco. The Carthaginians lost the territory in the Third Punic War to them. The Romans used the word *mauri* as a generic term for the diverse Muslim tribes living in the region. The Spaniards derived the name *moor* from it, which, in turn, was applied indiscriminately to all Arabs and North African aborigines. For reasons arcane to Dr. Jones, those chaps at Cunard were obsessed with naming their boats after ancient Roman provinces. In my current condition, I may be prone to verbosity, so do forgive my refreshing your awareness of things you may find humdrum.

The Cunard architects made her special. She was built with the newest high-tensile steel which resulted in weight reduction, which was not afforded to our sister ship, the *Lusitania*. Instead of wood, many of our steel decks were lined with corticene, a special cork cement/linoleum product. This material was used extensively on warships to minimize fire risk and save weight. The coal bunkers were placed along the outside of the ship, running its length to protect the vital interior components in case of war, lacking on the *Lusitania*. The four propellers were modified to make maximum use of our horsepower. Our two forward engines benefitted from two extra stages of turbine blades. *Lucy* missed out on these too; its four engines were identical. Envisage this: 780, 100 HP racing cars equaled the enormous pulling power of the 78,000 HP *Mauretania*, all those horses, and without the stable aroma.

Distinguished with the moniker *Maury the Magnificent,* she could be commandeered by the British Admiralty for war service. Our generous British Parliament had lent Cunard the money to build *Maury* and *Lucy*, and we were constructed for that possibility. Guns could be readily placed, for defense or attack, where people now played games or strolled at their leisure.

She tempered the waves better than her rivals, only when they were not in a foul mood of course. Beneath your feet you could feel the enormous power pulsating. She held the Blue Riband, an informal award for the fastest average speed, for twenty years, after setting the record in September,1909. She captured the prize from *Lusitania's* August, 1909, achievement, when she mastered the German ship *Deutschland*. In 1929, while I was serving aboard Cunard liner *Aquitania*, I read where the newly launched SS *Bremen* claimed the title for Germany. Our crew on the *Maury* was proud of the prestige accompanying the honor of being the fastest ship on the ocean. The bold blue pennant flying from the mast signified this fact.

> "When she was born in 1907, Maury was the largest thing ever put together by man. She always fascinated me with her graceful, yacht-like lines, her four enormous stacks, topped red funnels and her appearance of power and good breeding".
>
> —F.D.Roosevelt,
> Assistant Secretary, U S Navy

Truly, the ship was glorious for her time. As expected, I am devoted—she was my home. Forgive my drifting dialogue. I am somewhat unsettled momentarily—how do the French say it "Rattraper le temps perdue ", recapturing lost time I believe.

Our first voyage was hellish. Not that I have firsthand knowledge of Hades, but the haunt from which I was spirited away, rumors endure. The maiden crossing was the first week of November, the year was 1907. We were beset by persistently raging storms and nauseous passengers for the entire crossing. After docking at Cunard's Pier 54 and the travelers had gone ashore, one of the crew suggested I go dockside and look at the hull. I was startled to see a very sizable area near the starboard bow stripped clean of its black paint by the pounding breakers, right down to the bare gray metal.

Turbine steamships our size fear fog more than a severe hurricane. During a February storm in 1908, twenty miles out of New York, we were nearing the Cholera Banks (named by Captain Bebe as NYC was having a cholera epidemic when he found this new fishing spot). For a brief moment of clarity in the murkiness, our lookout spotted the strangest thing: a small sailing sloop that appeared to be aimless and in distress. His binoculars exhibited it sheltered three men. Remarkable for such a tiny craft to be that distant from shore in such weather.

Motion was observed and the alarm was sounded. In the rough seas, Captain Pritchard, instead of dispatching a rescue craft, maneuvered the 790-foot-long *Mauretania* between the floundering fishing boat and the oncoming waves, blanketing it from the wind. Ropes were thrown over the gunwale and the frozen fishermen were hauled aboard. The dory and its catch of iced cod were left as an offering to Triton.

In fifteen minutes the rescue was completed, and we were back on course for Liverpool. Two of the men were nearly dead from exhaustion and cold, but soon revived. Further treatment by me was not needed after the second day. The three rescued boaters went to England and back to America, the cost of the passage being funded by Cunard. Captain Pritchard received a fine pair of binoculars from President Teddy Roosevelt for deliverance of the three men. The lookout already had exceptional ones.

In March, a dreadful storm fell upon us. Five straight days we were buffeted about like driftwood. One giant wave eighty feet in height hit us on Tuesday, enveloping the bridge, damaging the chart house, and tearing a lifeboat from its rigging. Some of the sailors had minor injuries. Several were nearly swept away into the sea, but were saved by grasping the heavy iron railing. Captain Pritchard remarked it was the most beastly storm he had encountered. We docked twenty-four hours late.

Nothing is immune to ruckus. "FIGHT ON, THE *MAURETANIA*," proclaimed one headline. On one of the first June 1908 crossings, three Englishmen accused three Americans of cheating with loaded dice, which was found to be true. Following three consecutive days of cards and dice, a quarrel was probably inevitable. On Sunday the losers gathered to discuss their ill fortune. The winners came to collect on their IOUs, one for $385. Lives were threatened. A great brawl erupted, with flying cuspidors, match stands, glasses, bottles, and chairs tossed about in the ensuing commotion.

The ship's stewards restored the gentility to the smoking lounge. Six-schilling champagne definitely breaks down socially acceptable behavior where two-schilling medicinal waters may have led to a more diplomatic solution.

The Englishmen, not overjoyed at the outcome, sent wireless messages requesting detectives to meet them upon docking in New York. They wanted protection from the Americans should they fail to pay their IOUs. The Americans were arrested on the dock and taken into custody. Most puzzling to all concerned, the three Englishmen never showed to press charges, and the Americans never got their money. Captain Pritchard declared gambling could "not be stopped" on ships on the Atlantic Ocean.

I can call the spirits from the vasty deep.
—Shakespeare

Lodge 5787 17 September 1908 found us two days at sea outbound from Liverpool. I cannot recall how the recipients of the invitations to dinner that first night were chosen (innocents they were not), but I am sure general frivolity and being "one sheet to the wind" contributed. My required duties, inspecting the ship for health issues and checking on the passengers' wellness, could be burdensome each day. Professional obligations permitting, I was charged to banquet with those very same sojourners. I used my daily rounds to advantage, which permitted this roguish surgeon the opportunity to meet prospective invitees.

Miss Constance Collier, the famous British actress, a dark-haired beauty and every bit the effervescent stage star, arranged the inaugural feast with the headwaiter. I reserved the dining table next to the captain's in the first-class saloon with the second steward. Constance and I enlisted four jolly, itinerant souls that we hoped would make stimulating conversation. Maybe they would be of a kindred consciousness (or not).

What began as a friendly dinner party soon took on new dimensions when the founders decided these meetings should become a regular rite of passage. New novitiates would be engaged, oaths of secrecy would be administered, and a formal bacchanal would be held on the night of induction into the bohemian club. I was to preserve the record of the members and document the events of our gatherings. Thereupon the "Ancient and Select Order and Society of Heathens" was established. Physicians always trust laughter to be the best medicine.

Miss Collier was heading to America to star in the play *Samson* in New York, her first trip to the colonies. Her role as Cleopatra made her a legend on our side of the pond. The immensely respected actress decided to test her skills on Broadway. Undaunted and with her typical flair, she put our chefs to the test that first night. Maybe that is why it was such a splendid affair. Great food stirs the creative juices, especially when coupled with plentiful champagne. The Cotelettes d'Agneau a la Reforme (lamb) tasted superb and would satisfy the most discriminating palate, and the Perdeaux a la Constance Collier (partridge) was created especially for our hostess.

As we sipped cordials, we decided to have tribal names and marks, secret symbols known only to our fellow Heathens. Constance, quite naturally, became our HIGH PRIESTESS. Miss Alice Lloyd, an increasingly favored entertainer in America, adopted LITTLE MOTHER and placed a circle with a dot in the middle for her mark. Alice made a lasting first impression with her sky-blue eyes, blond hair, and natural smile enhanced by sparkling white teeth. You must be aware that these are the first things physicians observe in judging a person's, um, health.

Joining us at the table were Mr. Hugh Bellas, a self-contained, prosperous, and reserved Englishman—a lumber business promoter, I recollect. A much needed cultivated presence was Mr. Donald. G. Newton, who served on the board of directors of the Eye & Ear Hospital of New York. Both gentlemen were too shy or too stunned to participate in the proceedings with anything more than eating and conversation. They did sign their names to the menu, but failed to choose a tribal name or mark. Mr. Bellas had made his real mark in 1896 and onward when he traveled the continent with other lumbermen in an attempt to consolidate the various lumber mills under one corporation. In 1901, he allegedly formed the Redwood Trust in California.

In attendance was one English comedian, Mr. Tom McNaughton, who, along with his brother, Fred, was currently bringing their brand of English humor to the colonies. Tom was the husband of Miss Alice Lloyd. Upon docking they would begin rehearsals in the upcoming production of *The Bonnie Belles* in New York, as stars of the show. Actually that George Cohan play was later consigned to the shelf, but they would go on tour, playing the Grand Opera House in Syracuse, New York, in November. Tom picked the PHUNNY PHUNSTER for his secret name and a smiling cat for his mark.

Mr. Arthur L. Pearse, the always-on-the-move mining engineer, wanted to be the LITTLE CHIEF and was with a mark of two little ears. Finally, and without verbal objections I became BIG CHIEF, with a nose and whiskers as my mark, as I always sported a well-trimmed mustache. Forthwith: the Heathens were hatched. Entries were duly noted and archived in the sacred book.

After meeting Mr. and Mrs. McNaughton at supper I remembered a humorous story that I had noticed in an English paper months previous. With little effort, I am able to recall it in its entirety, the legal case of *McNaughton v. Holborn Borough Council* in Westminster, England. Alice was suing because of personal injuries (a bad cut on her forehead) and damages to her automobile in the accident. It involved that town having an unlit streetlamp. After leaving their show at Stratford, they were proceeding to the Trocadero, a London restaurant frequented by actors and the late-night crowd. Their chauffeur collided with the ill-lighted lamp, and Miss Lloyd was badly cut. Mr. McNaughton was in the witness box and was questioned.

"You are a comedian, I believe?"

"People say so," he replied (to laughter).

"Among your other successes, you married Miss Alice Lloyd."

"Yes, my greatest success," Tom replied (to more laughter).

"You were in the car when the accident happened?"

"Yes, I was looking straight ahead," said Tom.

"What time was it?"

"It struck twelve as we struck the lamppost," Tom replied (to more laughter).

The judge dismissed the case. Little Mother's forehead looked fine to the trained eyes of the Big Chief.

Our maiden conclave awakened the dark forces of nature to bear down on our ship later that evening. Abruptly, there was a loud noise, and the ship shuddered stem to stern in the most abnormal manner. This was especially worrisome since the ship was in the midst of fighting heavy seas and gale force winds, having caught the tail end of a West Indian hurricane 360 miles from Sandy Hook, New Jersey. This marked the entrance to the Ambrose Channel, the main shipping lane to New York.

The force of a detached propeller blade on the after-starboard side seemed to make the entire middle section of the ship rise up and buckle the floors. Power failed, the ship swung broadside into the waves and the seas washed over it. We soon learned that the wayward blade punctured the hull and that the pumps were pressed into service to keep out the cold Atlantic. The world's biggest liner had lost all turbine power and was foundering mid-ocean, pounded by mountainous waves. One of our steward's commented that the masts of the ship "quivered like bamboo fishing poles."

Passengers were thrown about their cabins and countless rushed screaming into the hallways. Due to the sudden shock and alarm, startled women emerged from their cabins scantily clad. With a doctor's professional eye I glimpsed a handful of ladies adorned with merely a chemise and a boa. You are aware that sailors have a hallowed tradition to perpetually accept naked women on their vessel; it brings good luck. Muttered among old time seamen is that women in clothes bring misfortune. Why does that conjure images of the *Wreck of the Hesperus* in my mind?

"ACTRESS PREVENTS PANIC," declared the headline in the *Taunton Courier*, 23 September 1908. Captain Pritchard attempted to reassure the passengers during the frenzy caused by the incident and ordered those in need of companionship to assemble in the café. Women fainted. People were visibly frightened, but not a complete rout yet. At the height of the crisis, our newly enshrined Little Mother, Alice Lloyd, stood up and began singing "Over the Hills and Far Away." She continued with other diverting songs for over an hour, while the ship rolled about at the mercy of the surging waves. Alice's inspiring voice sang away our fears. When the engines restarted, my confidence renewed, as if I had doubts.

Our new High Priestess, Miss Collier, gave Alice a kiss and Captain Pritchard thanked her warmly following her performance. Friday afternoon, when safely at anchor outside Sandy Hook, New Jersey, the captain regaled Alice in the main saloon. This was an esteemed honor because Captain Pritchard infrequently dined with travelers personally.

The *New York Times* called it the *hoodoo* trip. Captain Pritchard had lain to rest his beloved wife just days before our departure and was still bereaved. Truly one of the great captains, at twelve years old, he began as a twelve-shilling-a-week cabin boy rather than go to an orphanage, from cook to commodore of the Cunard fleet so to speak. Captain Pritchard retired in 1910 and married the manager of London's Mount Hotel, the highly regarded Katherine Parry.

After we were bashed about by the gale, almost making the ship turn turtle in the middle of the Atlantic Ocean, I had work to do. Fourteen stokers working in the coal bunkers were injured—not to awful, we quartered 385 of them. I tended to one broken arm and one broken leg, and one man needed twenty-three stitches to a laceration to his scalp. A hectic night for me, and the endless queue of seasick passengers contributed to my exhaustion.

Without resting, my next obligation was to sign the immigration forms. After every crossing I had to certify the health and sanity of each of my passengers. This process was done while the ship remained in quarantine, calmly at anchor a few miles from the pier prior to the wayfarers disembarking. The wording on the form might be of interest, entitled "Affidavit of Surgeon." I must swear to have made a "personal examination to the best of my knowledge and belief to be true and correct . . . all particulars relative to the mental and physical conditions of each alien", undoubtedly, exceptions needed to be extended to the Heathens. On numerous trips we ferried two thousand passengers and, notwithstanding my junior surgeon's assistance, the process takes a long time. After looking at a thousand faces I retired to my quarters. I drifted into that blissful sleep only sailors can take pleasure in, wondering how our feast had managed to arouse the wrath of Poseidon.

August 1909 found me assisting Chicago surgeon Louis McArthur in successfully performing an appendectomy on a young boy. Dr. McArthur was on his way to the Budapest Medical Congress when I appropriated his expertise. The seas were favorable and the ship did not have to be stopped during the surgery. I have observed that the human appendix seems aggravated by the sea and, notably, in bad weather.

Captains of the nearby rivercraft sounded their sirens in greeting the *Mauretania* as it approached its dock in New York after her record-breaking trip from Liverpool. Captain Pritchard, who customarily would have the ship respond in kind, neglected to do so. Mrs. Isaac Rice, president of the Anti-Noise Society, was shaking a disapproving finger of warning at the good captain. 21 August 1909.

On 26 December 1909, Alice Lloyd, nearly mid-ocean on the *Mauretania*, received a wireless message from Broadway agent Martin Beck. Producers Klaw and Erlanger had released her from the contract because Alice was displeased with the arrangement. Mr. Beck, recognizing the opportunity, immediately contacted her with a new proposal, which included her husband, Tom, and his brother, Fred, as the opening act. He signed her by wireless. To perform four songs, two times a day, for $1,500 per week, Alice agreed to the terms. Miss Lloyd was now the highest-paid actress in vaudeville.

It is a rare thing indeed to get a stowaway on the *Maury*. It is more unusual when he is a famous attorney. Most of his fame arose from his representation of the wealthy, albeit mentally unstable, Harry Thaw, who killed Sanford White, the famous architect, in 1906. The first trial resulted in a hung jury, not the defendant. In the second trial his counselor invoked Attorney Delphin Delma's "by reason of insanity" defense, the dementia Americana, or the sanctity of home and wife argument. And that defense worked. Thaw spent seven years, on and off, in an asylum. Sanford was killed over his romance with Evelyn Nesbit, Thaw's wife. (Dare I say a true femme fatale?) The name of Thaw's attorney was Martin W. Littleton, and he was in a big hurry to get to London, so he had a *brainstorm*, a word first coined at the first Thaw trial.

In May 1910, unable to purchase a ticket, Littleton just waltzed on board. It must have been a waltz; any other type of dance step would have aroused suspicion. He mingled with the other passengers until we were two hours out of New York harbour. "It was very important that I should be in London at this time, and I determined to come over, if possible, as a paying stowaway. To accomplish this, I simply walked on board. Then I was discovered and could not be dropped overboard, so the best was made of the matter," he said.

Littleton would become more famous defending Harry Sinclair in the Teapot Dome scandal in 1927. Amazingly, Sinclair was only convicted of contempt of court for hiring private detectives to shadow his jurors, being sentenced to six months in jail after Littleton took it to the Supreme Court in 1929. Mr. Littleton was truly a man blessed with *furor loquendi*, though the crew would politely say "blarney." Wandering around the deck one day out from Liverpool, I asked the crewmen what they were doing with a substantial length of rope. After my playful pestering they informed me of their intention to keelhaul the ticketless hitcher since the Captain refused to use his "daughter" on him for a well-deserved flogging. I pointed out to them he was merely a stowaway attorney, not a pirate, whereupon they added an extra length of rope.

Conveying furtive strangers is becoming customary. Bound for England in March 1910, an escaped criminal was found traveling under an alias. Frenchman Adrian Maderian, convicted of attempted murder, was heading home. Wouldn't it have been quite the event had we invited him to our initiation supper—imagine the tales. He had escaped from the prison in French Guiana, readily identified by its name of Ile du Diable (Devil's Island). This was his fourth escape, making it to the United States. What panache he had to have made it this far. He was removed in irons at Liverpool. I wondered why he was obsessed with going home after escaping. Seeking vengeance, or retribution for being falsely accused?

Outbound; Liverpool to New York, Day II

"Because he should knowe howe the time went away":
Thomas Percy's reason he gave Guy Fawkes
his watch to time
the lighting of the fuse for the failed Gunpowder
Plot in 1605.

Tempus really does fugit, although not for me physically any longer. Tempus's passing always goes unnoticed, and it has always vexed me that we only seem to miss it after it has "fugited" irretrievably. It has been nearly two years since our first baptism by tempest. Maybe the events of the first night made us more respectful toward the gods of the seas.

One November 1910 was designated for the gathering of the tribe. The High Priestess presided over the table with her usual regal aplomb. Miss Collier organized a spectacular dining experience. Most Heathens and novitiates had a menu item named after them. Two other founders present, besides Miss Collier, were Little Chief, Arthur Pearse, and me, Big Chief. Allow me to introduce the infidels according to their menu items. Always bear in mind, God sends meat, and the devil sends cooks.

Aperitif Bonne Humeur
Caviar Grande Priestess
Freyda Sole
Constance en Consomme
Tornado May BlaYnay
Mouette Bainbridge
Dolce von Ostheim
Debattre Salade MacMahon
Bonne Bouche Grand Chef
Glace Oom Cum
Frommage Pivvy

Fruit Sinkit
Puite d' Amour Leon XIV
Café Heathen
Pousse Café Le Amiamo Tutte

Embellishments may seem unfamiliar, but anything made in a cauldron in our galley becomes sublime. "Oom cum pivvy sinkit" are the words to our not-so-secret toast recited before imbibing a cocktail (actually an aberration of an old English slang expression, but we liked the sound). 'Twas a grand meal, although one really had to trust the culinary skills of the chef as the ingredients would seem more suited to an elegant druid ritual (reasonably, the chef eliminated the mistletoe). Mentioning rituals, you will now be privy our secret rites, printed for the very first time, and the last. You will find them not as ensanguined as the aforesaid druids, and since it is the sixth day of the moon, you may safely read them.

Rites to Be Observed at Initiation Ceremonies of the Ancient and Select Order of Heathens

To those assembled before me, the Big Chief of the
Ancient Order of Heathens,
in virtue of which rank I am entitled to admit novitiates
into the circle, be it known
that such meetings must be approached with all the
seriousness and decorum
worthy of the ancient order, and any lapse or infringement
may be dealt with
at a fitting time by the council in conclave assembled.
Clasp the hands behind
the head, cross the left foot over the right, incline the head
forward, and face
downward.

Three obeisances to the fetish.

You will now repeat after me the Declaration of the Oom
Cum Pivvy Tribe,
by which name members are known to one another.

And I promise and affirm that on this, my initiation as a noviate in the Ancient
and Select Order and Society of Heathens, that I will uphold their tenets according
to the best of my abilities, keep the objects of their society secret as also the signs
of their society by which they are known, one unto the other, and which they employ
for various ceremonies. After each of the following *obligations*, you will repeat after me
the prescribed answer.
Will you promise to act up to, in every way, to the best of your power
the rules of the society as an novitiate?
Answer "Oom Cum."
Will you always do your best to help forward with a loving hand
your fellow Heathens and others worthy or in distress?
Answer "Pivvy."
Will you promise never to drink more than may be good for you at one time?
Answer "Sinkit."
Will you promise that you will always return answer
to the Heathen signs of greeting immediately and under whatever circumstances
you may see them and likewise the signs that relate to your health?
Answer "Oom cum pivvy sinkit."

Three obeisances to the fetish.

Kneel therefore on the left knee and give the sign of greeting to the Heathen fetish:
arms to the sides, forearms flexed, fingers separated.
This is the order of greeting when Heathen meets Heathen and must
only be given in public without the genuflection, which is solely reserved for the Idol

of the Ancient Order. This sign signifies that I embrace
you with all my heart.
When given this sign, a Heathen must at once reply under
any and every circumstance
by placing the spread fingertips below the lobes of the ears
with elbows in direct line
with the shoulders, signifying, full up to the ears with
human kindness, love to all fellow
Heathens and anything else that may seem good, except
all such excesses that
would violate the spirit of good Heathenship.
Rise duly obligated, *sister*. Rise duly obligated, *brother*.
And we will now complete our instruction of the signs and
ceremonies.

The Toast

Take glass in right hand, raise it level of your lip, and utter
the symbolic words "Oom cum."
Await the prescribed reply, "Pivvy." And then in unison,
with the toasted one
or one's whisper of "Sinkit," and proceed.

The Silent Toast

Raise glass in left hand to left ear and thence to right ear,
from whence
it is carried to the mouth.

Gadzooks! If you survived this unauthorized reading, you must now forget the befuddled stanzas, or use them at your own risk. A plague of five days kinetosis upon thee if thou betray them, let us return to the celebration.

Not the gathering of flawless souls one would at first perceive, although a few were very prominent members of normal society that had strayed to a disturbed mental state for an evening of revelry. Tribal initiates this night were May Blayney, a charming actress, fresh from her lavishly lauded role in London's Wyndham's Theater production of *The Little Damozel.* She had the "gift of genuine pathos," according to one critic. Her path now led to New York to star in *The Importance of Being Earnest.* The recently married actress Countess Von Ostheim and Fred (FREYDA) Harrison, actor/manager of the Haymarket Theater in London, were in attendance.

> In 75 test cases of insane persons
> it was found that alcoholism on the part of one or
> both parents was the cause of their derangement.
> —R. Watchorn, The White Slave Traffic, 1910

Dignifying the table was Robert Watchorn, former union mining leader and recently retired commissioner of immigration at Ellis Island, who had recently entered the oil business. His biography of an impoverished eighteen-year-old coming to America, starting his life there as a coal miner and his rise to prominence and success, is a fascinating book, nearly being arrested on his first day in America. The dispute was over currency exchange rates for a doughnut.

William Seamen Bainbridge (MOUSIE) a renowned cancer surgeon, found himself entangled in our web and added an agreeable erudite presence, along with Fulton McMahon, a prominent NYC attorney. Fulton would befriend Dr. Bainbridge this night, and they would return to the Pulteney Hotel in Bath, England, three weeks for the cure at its spas.

Last but not least were my assistant surgeon Joseph A. Corbitt (CUPID CHERUB), along with Shirley S. Lloyd (SHIRLEY) and Mr. Leon Garcey. Leon was in railroads and represented French ventures in the United States. Much more will be forthcoming about Mr. Garcey at a later date, but I will say his name was much longer and his interests were, let me say, quite diverse.

A dapper, slender lad, the Princeton educated Fulton McMahon had, in 1894, been instrumental in the removal from office of District Attorney John Fellows in New York. The reason was "Failure of speedy trials in murder cases." He wrote a straightforward book on the War Revenue Act of 1898. Funding the Spanish-American war with tax dollars was of no concern of the Big Chief.

After an illustrious legal career in New York, he moved back to his hometown of Cambridge, Ohio, upon the passing of his brother. He resided in the family home with his widowed sister-in-law, Ada. Prying minds should be reminded of his Heathen oath. In 1934, while doing work in the front yard of that home, a car parked on the curb, driven by John Campbell of Kansas City, who had his wife as a passenger. Fulton, upset with the loud radio, shouted for him to turn it down. Mr. Campbell refused, wherein Mr. McMahon turned his flowing hose upon the couple. As Mr. Campbell got out and attempted to grab the hose's nozzle, Fulton tripped over the tangled tube and fell down, striking his head on the concrete walk. Rushed to the hospital, he died hours later, a bizarre, sad, and premature end for our tribal brother.

> You will notice that since women began to discard one petticoat after another, and appear finally in the scantiest of skirts, they have lost a great deal of the outward respect and consideration which used to be shown them in days of fuller petticoats.
>
> —May Blayney, *El Paso Herald*, 23 October 1912

The newspapers never spelled her name correctly, at times omitting the middle *y*. And I know not why since she was so popular at the turn of the last century. Young May began on the stage in San Francisco with the Alcazar Stock Company in the play *Quo Vadis* with good reviews. Mrs. Chinn, being married to Richard Chinn at the time, skedaddled when a judgment by default was rendered against her for not repaying a promissory note of $125 owed to Mr. A. M. Shields, manager of the Equitable Life Insurance Co. She "persistently refused to pay him back." Mr. Shields was an excellent marksman at the Olympic Gun Club and had won awards for shooting live birds, but this pigeon flew away with his money.

Hightailing it towards England, she learned an English accent, and triumphantly returned to America for her Broadway debut as an English girl playing in the *Walls of Jericho* at the Savoy Theater in New York. Returning to her dressing room between acts, she caught a thief ransacking her handbag. May yelled for assistance and grabbed the burglar. Police were summoned and A. M. Shields was arrested with seventeen dollars in his possession, the exact amount May had previously had in her purse. Big Chief could not resist; not millionaire Mr. Shields but rather one Frank Hamill.

After marrying English actor A. E. Matthews in 1909, May's star shone brighter. First, she appeared in *Chantecler* as a very pretty hen pheasant. Was Mr. Shields in the audience? Then she starred in *Man and Superman*. Moreover, she found time to have and raise a daughter and twin sons, divorcing English actor Alfred Matthews in 1918. Mr. Matthews had the dubious distinction of being the only actor banned from acting in G. B. Shaw's plays by the great man himself for "tampering with the lines."

Most people know how superstitious female actors can be. May bequeathed to fellow Heathen Miss Constance Collier her little white ivory elephant, which had brought her so much good luck in *Chantecler*. Hopefully it would bring the same to the High Priestess, who was opening as the sinner Thais in the eponymous play in New York. The good luck must have been exhausted as the play only ran for thirty-one performances. In Miss Collier's defense, the play went on a long US and Canadian tour, and Mr. Beerbohm Tree produced it later in London. A remnant of enchantment truly must have remained in the little charm after all.

For reasons obscure to me, May found her way to Orange Free State, South Africa, after leaving the stage in 1922, dying there in 1953. She enjoyed gardening and breeding English bulldogs in her new country. *Variety* magazine kindly referred to her as a former legit actress, but I thought she really was named appropriately on the menu as Tornado with Sauce Droisegaux (bird sauce).

You may not think that much money could be made in wallpaper—a ship's surgeon would rarely think about such a thing. Presently returning from England, Shirley Sabin Lloyd had inherited a small importing company upon the death of her husband in 1892. She envisioned a bigger future for those wall coverings and now owned one of the largest importers of the aforementioned product in the United States.

She was one of the two daughters of Joseph Sabin and Mary Winterborne Sabin. Until his passing in 1881, Joseph was one of the most noted bibliophiles and booksellers in the United States. His knowledge and ability to recognize collecting value were legendary around the world. His business acumen must have inspired Shirley to turn the small shop at 2609 Broadway, New York, into branch stores in Boston, Newark, Chicago, and affiliates across the United States. I now admire wallpaper whenever onshore.

The audience is nothing but the 4th wall in a room
and it is often well papered.
—Mlle. Edvina, opera star, 1912

Constance Collier, Heathen High Priestess, this night informed the heedful throng of one of her personal rituals. Upon her pincushion at her dressing table was pinned a little black bogey made of rags and thread. If she was successful in a new part, the mascot's impish face would bear a cheerful grin, but if the show failed, the creature would scowl. All those within earshot surreptitiously checked their clothing for any loose fibers.

Now, if I mention *electrical engineer*, you may think we had very little voltage at our table this night. You would be wrong. Since 1906, Constance had been married to Julian LeStrange, who was educated at Oxford in things electric. Walking onto the stage at the Lyceum Theater in London one day, he did an impromptu audition, and soon, the handsome young actor was only electrifying audiences. They first met on Mount Olympus. Three years prior, in Herbert Tree's production of *Ulysses*, Constance had the lead role as Athena, and Julian was cast as Mercury, and they had the first scene together. Having a flirtation with one of Calypso's nymphs at the time he scantly heeded the heavenly Athena.

Our Miss Collier had disavowed marriage, undeterred by relentless suitors. Rumors of her ongoing romance with fellow Heathen Sir Beerbohm Tree were whispered. Olivia Truman, Sir Tree's resolute confidant, witnessed them entering London's Carlton Hotel for afternoon tea, and fixed his gaze toward Constance as if he could "eat her with rapture!" England's most famous comic entertainer, Dan Leno, (Constance told us he yearned to play Shakespeare), offered her an eye catching diamond brooch one night as an engagement gift. When Constance refused the keepsake, he left and gave it to a nearby barmaid while he quaffed his rejection away.

In the midst of her run in the play, *Oliver Twist*, she did get married. Julian LeStrange secured a marriage license with a date of three weeks hence, surprising her at supper one night. They both laughed and thought it a great joke until the weeks had elapsed and Julian reminded her of their appointment at the church on Thursday. On the designated morning, she woke up with no intention of getting married. "Invisible chains seemed to drag me!" she exclaimed. She hailed a cab and sped to her wedding, finding Julian waiting. Vows were taken, and on this day, both were an hour late to their respective afternoon matinees. After her evening performance, Julian was waiting at the stage door for her, and they drove to a little hotel. The romantic wedding supper was cold ham and red wine.

Miss Collier would say her marriage was like an intermittent love affair and that Julian had the moods of an April day. They spent most of their time apart. Julian had a successful acting career but was always overshadowed by his wife's greater achievements in England. Off to America they went, where he was cast opposite Maxine Elliott—"Too often," it was whispered. Mr. LeStrange regularly found himself on opposite ends of the American continent from his wife.

When war began he joined the Royal Canadian Flying Corps for one and a half years, where abnormal high blood pressure unfitted him from active service. Ironically, he died while acting with his wife in her 1918 New York production of *An Ideal Husband*. Near the end Julian received wonderful reviews and had the great success he so desired. 1918 was the tragic year of the Spanish influenza, the great pandemic that killed over fifty million people, mostly young adults. After a brief bout with the contagious disease, followed by pneumonia, he succumbed to the illness. Or maybe the Three Fates, Clotho, Lachesis, and Atropos, decided the High Priestess's bogey had been allotted enough life giving threads.

"She cost the throne," disclosed the headline in newspapers around the world. Maybe her presence, and, notoriously anticipated arrival by New York's leading socialites, hastened our journey across the pond. The *Maury* set the record this crossing. Allow me to introduce the freshly minted Countess Von Ostheim, a dazzling beauty and our most celebrated guest this fine November evening. (Don't take my word for it, read the newspapers.) Formerly, her name was Wanda Lottero, a dancer in *The Merry Widow* theater production in London. Years earlier, she had won a beauty contest in Milan and was crowned the Loveliest Woman in Italy. Supposedly, her beau and future husband, Prince Hermann of Saxe-Weimar, duke of Saxony, had gotten her the part in *The Merry Widow*, a story circulating among other actors.

The prince was a notorious womanizer, gambler, and generally a royal deadbeat of the German principality. His parents were continuously paying off his debts, and it routinely made the newspapers. In defense of the prince, the second son of a grand duke rarely gains the throne. The prince was recently given the boot in his courtship of Marie Bonaparte, a glamorous and well-dowered young lady. Her father, who owned part of the casino in Monte Carlo, was insulted by the rumors and news accounts of the misbehaving prince's relentless pursuit of Miss Lottero in London. His daughter giving the poor prince money was equally biting. Marie was an overtly libidinous lady, being a psychoanalyst and friend of Sigmund Freud. Under the pseudonym A. J. Narjani, she publish the outcome of a lengthy and exhaustive study in the journal *Bruxelles-Medical.* The topic was frigidity and centimeters in women, 2.5 or less being optimal for volupte.

Rebuked by Marie, the young prince married the blossoming Miss Lottero, before he squandered all of his options I deduced. The bylines in the papers stated the marriage was morganatic, wherein he renounced all claims and rights to succession to the throne. He was corralled by his horrified parents, with his debts paid and allotted a monthly stipend. Naturally, his family was disappointed in his choice of wife, and most likely, he did not care. Having spent just one evening with his exquisite Paola unmasked a most captivating young lady, more a princess than Hermann was a prince. She exuded a stately mien, and we were proud to initiate her into the clan. Besides, her father was a merchant sea captain.

Provocative, charming, clever, and exquisite, the twenty-one-year-old princess combined all of them in a wonderful medley. She spoke with the most beguiling French-accented English I have ever heard, almost musical. Her husband most notably was not accompanying her on this crossing, and on this, their first anniversary, made the miscreant gaggle gossip. Princess Paola told us of her busy social schedule that would begin upon her arrival in America. She would not have one day to herself as invitations to social events would keep her endlessly occupied. Americans may have gotten rid of the king, but many of them court the royals socially, with vigor, especially a new, refreshing, and prominent one. Her presence that evening was truly enjoyed and will be long remembered.

Although we set the transatlantic speed record this crossing (27.5 knots), we were robbed of the elapsed time record by a blinding snowstorm off Long Island, which delayed our arrival in New York. In our era, the competition between the fastest steamships was momentous and published whenever a new record occurred. Multiple bets were made on each voyage. Wagers were made on everything: speed per day, miles per day, and end-of-cruise average speed and duration. Frequently, large sums of money were in play among the well-to-do first-class passengers. I always thought the more nonsensical bet would have been the actual tonnage of coal we burned each day (roughly 1,200, depending on speed). Unnoted was that it took twenty trains of twenty coal cars each to give the ship enough coal to travel from Liverpool to New York and return. It only requires a little blizzard to be the cause of a plunger to either lose money or make money on the high seas.

Princes Paola von Ostheim revision: I recently read the headlines of a Parisian periodical: "LOSES WIFE WHO COST THE THRONE." The countess was getting divorced. The grounds were nonsupport, infidelity (how did she imagine otherwise), and cruelty. The evidence showed he relied entirely upon her for his support—mainly financial and not spiritual, it appeared. She was granted the dissolution in Paris in July 1911. Predictably, that marriage did not last long. Always catching the wandering eyes of European royalty, the princess soon became involved with King Constantine I of Greece, who found her equally irresistible as Prince Hermann had a few short years earlier. Years later, while stationed on my new ship, the *Aquitania*, I read that she had written a book about the Greek king after his death. The book contained the publishable portion of the written correspondence of their ten-year liaison. Ah, what a woman she was!

One night in September 1910 became suspenseful when we received a wireless message to search, and hopefully, rescue survivors of a sinking ship. The British tramp steamer *West Point* had an engine-room fire on 27 August. The ship was bound for Savannah, Georgia, with a load of fertilizer. Attempts to contain the fire failed and late in the day on the twenty-eighth, Captain Pinkham gave the order to lower the lifeboats away from the stricken ship. The lifeboats stood by the vessel as it burned, and later, the crew attempted to retrieve food and water. One of the crew later remarked that the flames were too intense and the red-hot decks prevented him from securing provisions for the boats. The ship finally sank. The two surviving boats became separated, the other safely rescued by the steamer *Devonian*.

On a black night six days later, while battling rough seas and gale force winds, our lookout spotted a glowing red rocket handheld by one of the men in the lifeboat. Our crew proceeded to recover Captain Pinkham and fifteen other crewmen, all in good health, despite being hungry, thirsty, and extremely cold. I did treat several men for burns, and Captain Pinkham had a dislocated shoulder that needed attention.

He described how incessant bailing had kept his lifeboat afloat. Captain Pinkham told us he had given up hope of being rescued and had been navigating toward the Azores, a group of nine volcanic islands eight hundred miles west of continental Portugal. Bless that rocket.

A fund-raiser held for the salvaged sailors garnered $450 from our passengers. Intense bidding for an eight-week-old white Persian cat Captain Pinkham had saved from his foundering ship raised one hundred dollars as well. The cat's black sibling was in the other rescued lifeboat. One of the *West Point*'s crew reflected, "I wish we had a couple dozen such cats."

A. Einstein received assorted blows on his face tonight in the smoking room. 29 October 1910, and the ship was in quarantine off New York City. Two loud smacks were heard. A tall young man in a gray suit was seen walking away from a much-shorter man whose hair was ruffled. Mr. Einstein reported the incident to the chief steward, but he had not witnessed the incident, nor had anyone else, it seems. Neither party would respond to the inquiries of reporters who happened to be on the ship, looking for juicy gossip. The alleged assailant, Mr. McMillan, later said he was angered at comments Mr. Einstein had made in regard to the mathematics in games of chance. Einstein's face appeared as rosy as the carpet on the floor.

"SURGERY DONE AT TWENTY-SIX KNOTS," affirmed the headlines on 26 November 1910. Huge rollers caused by a gale were bouncing us about. Six-foot-four, 300-pound Baron Hermann von Eckardstein of Berlin, after a night of liberal drinking and eating, had an abdominal pain and requested my opinion. I immediately recognized the symptoms of a ruptured appendix. Providentially, acclaimed abdominal surgeon, Dr. Frederick Coerr, was in transit. He kindly performed the operation, while I assisted, and my second, fellow Heathen Dr. J. Frank Nicholson, administered the ether. The patient not only survived but was able to immediately resume his duties at the German Embassy after a short stay at the Dr. Bull Sanitarium. Heathens can be doctors, and not of the witch variety.

After this favorable outcome, I was extremely relieved. In July 1909, we had lost one of our crew, Robert Gibbon, a coal stoker from Liverpool. Suffering from an abdominal pain Mr. Gibbon had ignored the symptoms a tad too long. We rushed him to surgery, but he died. Again, I had the assistance of two New York doctors who were passengers, Dr. Francis Kinnicutt and Dr. Walter James. Mr. Gibbon was buried at sea. The passengers collected five hundred dollars for his widow. I hoped this would be the end of internal operations at sea.

Subsequently, upon removing the offending organ from our celebrated German patient, I surveyed the ruptured mass, and divined the past and future of our dear perfumed parlor snake, the Baron von Eckardstein. I knew the present well enough, which leads us to a brief departure from the narrative.

The Baron's great friendship with Kaiser Wilhelm II of German led to his appointment to the court of King James in London in 1895. There, the dashing diplomat met, courted, and won the heart of Grace Blundell Maple, only daughter and heir of Sir John Maple, the extraordinarily wealthy furniture dealer. "EUROPE'S LOVE STORY," the headline announced when they were married in 1896.

"VON ECKARDSTEIN VS. VON ECKARDSTEIN," touted the headline in 1907, divorce English style versus German style. In the German court the baron sought divorce for wifely disobedience; she sued him for restitution of conjugal rights in the English court. The English court dismissed the claim that the German court took precedence. A divorce was granted for proof of desertion. The heart of the matter was Sir Maple's will and the inheritance he had placed in trust for Grace. He died suddenly in 1903. Knowing his future son-in-law to be a notorious gambler of stock, turf, and cards, he desired for his daughter to be financially protected. He had previously paid off one million dollars of the baron's debts before the marriage.

Sir Maple loathed the thought of restoring an impecunious German family to prominence, especially with his fifteen-million pounds of hard-earned English money. A stipulation in the will stated that for 240 days of the year, the couple must reside in the United Kingdom, and the baron would receive fifteen thousand dollars in "pin" money as his stipend. That was a posthumous and deliberate insult from the deceased Sir Maple. Try as the baron and baroness would, they could not succeed in breaking the trust.

In true-to-form German retaliation, the baron invoked every conceivable means to hurt his wife, including cruel treatment, insulting sarcasm, and even threatened suicide. The threat had credence as he had, in his youth, during the wee hours of the morning, jumped from a second-story window at the Metropolitan Club in Washington, DC. He won the wager without physical injury.

Baroness Grace, notwithstanding her social rank, was quite the fertile debauchee. She bore four children, the first-named Kit to the Baron Hermann, Reginald with Dr. C. J. Williams in 1906, and Heather with Elidor Campbell, while married. The last two would be discreetly adopted out. Finally, she had Priscilla with her second husband, Archibald Weigall, in 1914. At one point the Baron's friend, German Chancellor Wilhelm, deliberated Hermann's dismissal from the diplomatic corps for his misbehaviors. If not for Wilhelm's failure to do so, our story, to the reader's reprieve, might have ended here.

"Baroness von Eckardstein dead," alleged the headline in September 1912. My first thought was that the removal of his appendix may have been a mistake. During a wild boar hunt, the baroness was shot and killed by her kinsman Count Finch von Eckardstein. I soon realized it was the Baron's sister.

Heathens wrote books, several memorable, but none so terrible to deserve imprisonment. In 1913, von Eckardstein, while he was the chargé d'affaires in London, suggested a triple alliance between Great Britain, Germany, and Japan. Germany was anti-English, but, for a brief, convoluted reason, considered the idea. Count Hayashi of Japan insisted Germany be omitted while under intense British pressure for German inclusion. In fact, there almost was an Anglo-German alliance in 1913. What a difference that political entente would have made at that juncture in history, especially to the French.

The year 1914 found our baron a slighted and injured man. He was prepared to publish a volume entitled *Reminiscences and Memorable Political Occurrences*, allegedly to contain numerous secret documents and reveal damaging political plots. The entire contents and proofs were seized by the German police. Hermann was arrested, incarcerated, and threatened with dire consequences two days after the declaration of war. An obscure spy for the fatherland, he had conducted secret missions as an active agent, and his name was associated with political intrigues in Europe as well as America. None ever were acknowledged to be of any consequence.

The year 1915 found him languishing in solitary confinement at Magdeburg Prison. In 1918 the baron was released and dismissed from the diplomatic corps. The ever plotting Baron later wrote various books that were published without incident. I saved his life so he could fight against us. Blessed be the Hippocratic Oath. Next time you lay bare an appendix, take a good look.

Forgive my medical and mental distractions. I find myself rambling on without fealty for chronological accuracy. Since my return, time seems to pass with a strange ambiguity. This recently acquired affliction sometimes finds the good surgeon losing his mental compass.

Why Men Stare
Dr. Sydney Jones of the *Aquitania*, who is retiring
after thirty-six years of sea service, was talking about
time's changes. He thought the greatest change
was in women's dress and, on the subject, said wittily,
"It isn't the clothes that make men stare.
It's the girl that should be in them."
Greenfield Daily Reporter
March 12, 1931

December was always the most special month for crossings on the *Mauretania*. Holiday travelers were returning home to their welcoming families on both sides of the Atlantic. Others were on shopping sprees or merely enjoying the season abroad. The fireplaces in the cabins were well provisioned with firewood for the chilly journey, and the ship was festooned stem to stern with holiday decorations. December 1910 would be a hectic month aboard the merry *Maury*.

Homeward: New York to Liverpool, Day IV

On 3 December 1910, recruitment was sparse, but one celebrity at the table compensated for the lack of devotees with delicious tales of her romances and guile. Let me introduce Ellen Pauline Nathan Polly Chase, the famous actress, most noted for her revered leading role in J. M. Barrie's production of *Peter Pan*.

Joining her would be Jessie G. Hale, a vivacious woman who acted and owned a vaudeville theater company, most noted for introducing the child actor Baby Sheldon in 1908. In 1892, Mrs. Hale, formerly recognized by her stage name Donatha Lewis, filed a $950,000 breach of promise suit against James W. Paige, manufacturer of the Paige typesetting machine. She left the stage, moved to Hartford, Connecticut, and lived as his wife for a number of years. On April 22, the mutually agreed-upon day, they were to leave for Milwaukee and be married. At the final hour, Mr. Paige accused her of flirting with other men, calling off the wedding. He must have been the better actor of the two.

Rounding out the assemblage were J. Frank Nicholson, doctor by day, Heathen by night; Cedric Chivers, book publisher; and myself, Dr. Jones, alias, Big Chief.

Mr. Cedric Chivers was a distinguished fellow. Born in England, he left home as a youngster to learn the bookbinding trade, first in London then Paris. After gaining proficiency in that occupation, he invented several notable patents for reinforcing the bindings of books. The real fortune he told us came from his invention of the *vellucent* process of book-cover ornamentation. I saw one, and the result was elegant. The decorated bindings would become prized to collectors. The rebinding of library books and schoolbooks was very profitable, he said, as these were in constant need of refurbishing. He opened Chivers Bookbinding Co. in Brooklyn, New York, in 1909, and visited his facility when he could. At this time, he was currently town mayor of Bath, England, a title he would keep for thirty years. I later came across an article stating that Cedric had crossed the pond round-trip 120 times in his lifetime, sadly not in our company again.

The most alluring Heathen seated at the table was Miss Pauline Chase. She signed her full name to the page: Ellen Pauline Nathan Chase. Not sure why. Everyone knew her. A beloved publicity darling of her time, reporters followed every drama, on and off the stage. She was most famous for her acclaimed role as Peter in the London production of the J. M. Barrie play *Peter Pan*.

The latest prattle I had seen in print before we sailed for Liverpool concerned her engagement to Claude Grahame-White, the famous English aviator. More provocative, he was traveling on the ship. Denials of the engagement by both parties had been printed in the newspapers, although several reported they had been secretly married. Yet here Mr. Grahame-White was, his planes stowed securely below in the ship's hold. *Of what purpose was an aeroplane if it had to be transported by a ship across the ocean,* how little foresight we possessed. Pauline was sailing to England to reprise her role as Peter Pan in what she admitted will be her last stage appearance.

Triumphs being few for the Heathen's, we counted Miss Chase's participation at our table for one evening an impressive success. The young lady was very much in demand socially, but she graciously accepted our invitation. Conversation flowed smoothly until an unnamed person asked her to tell the pink pajama story. She demurred at first. Then Cedric Chivers queried her about J. M. Barrie, the author of *Peter Pan.* Allegedly, Mr. Barrie and Ellen Terry, the most famous English actress, had legally adopted Pauline.

The rumor was that Barrie had wanted to marry Pauline when he divorced. Pauline said Mr. Barrie and his wife (not Miss Terry) had been living in an unhappy marriage and exploring adoption but were afraid because" one never knows how the child would turn out". Pauline, alone and living in London, was charming the audiences in his London production of the play. A strong friendship grew between her and Mr. Barrie, and what better person to adopt than a heretofore grown child. A proven quantity, if you will. At her baptism in 1909, Ellen Terry, the actress, and J. M. Barrie, the playwright, became her godparents. When Barrie's divorce was final (he would have been a prequalified Heathen) rumors circulated he wanted to marry Pauline, yet she denied that was ever a possibility, and she remained close friends with Barrie. One whisper put to slumber.

The next story must have been coaxed forth by the conviviality of the amiable company. Most of us had read how Pauline loathed telling of the pajamas, having gone so far as to legally suppress all images of her in those very same PJ's that had started her on the road to fortune and fame. She publicly became indignant at the mere mention of them. What a difference a night among the Heathens can make.

Opening night, 30 September 1902, Hoyt's Theater, NYC, an opportune chorus girl, the last one of seven girls cast for the dormitory scene in *The Liberty Belles,* took the stage. Call it what you will. At times, one simple thing can change your life forever. Pauline came onstage in pink pajamas (customarily girls always wore nightgowns, while men wore the pajamas) covered in ribbons and frills in the scene where the girls engage in a pillow fight.

She admitted that after becoming engaged by the company to play the role, she approached the author, Harry B. Smith, future Heathen Robert's brother. She suggested her favorite garment of comfort, her pink pajamas, instead of the nightgowns described in the book. He said, "Why not?" When she sat down at the piano and played a song at the end of the scene, she would become a part of theater lore for a generation. She was unprepared for the audience's response and, even less so, the public's as the pink pajamas become the rage of the day across America. Little girls wrote to Miss Chase, asking about them. She confided to still dressing in the original PJs every now and then. Not bad for a Washington, DC, girl, straight from the convent of the Sisters of the Holy Cross at sixteen, from the chorus line to worldwide acting fame by twenty-one.

I proposed allowing the Pauline "Polly" Chase story to end there, but felt obliged to disclose later news reports. Our feminine feline was engaged nine times—yes, nine. The list exposed a who's who of society from both sides of the Atlantic. First in line was the young Harvard student William Kibbe when she was sixteen; he trailed her to every show. Alexander Dow, the thirty-two year old printing press manufacturer was second. The year 1902 brought in Mr. Harold VanHorst, but never formally announced, followed by George Cannon, a New York banker's son. The Honorable Arthur Wellesley, son of the duke of Wellington, claimed 1904. London soldier and publisher Walter Limpus became cannon fodder after 1905. English millionaire sportsman Nicolas Wood bagged 1906 briefly for his trophy room. Aviator Claude Grahame-White flew through 1910 and early 1911, although judging by shipboard behavior, not readily apparent to me or the crew. The Claude-Chase saga ceased in May 1911, she jilted him and broke the engagement.

At the Carlton Hotel in London, fellow Heathen and actress Irene Fenwick would play a role in that disengagement after a trip across on our little dinghy. The reason (and I quote Pauline) is as follows: "Yes, there is no unpleasantness. I concluded Mr. Graham-White could not compensate me in my retirement from the stage. And please do not report that I am engaged to anyone else." Claude did go on to be one of the most famous of the early aviators. And the winner of the engagement marathon in 1914 was Alexander Drummond, wealthy son of a London banker. Polly wanted security. She married him and bore three wonderful children, and they lived happily ever after as she wished. As Peter would have said in the play, "You just think wonderful thoughts, and they will lift you up in the air." Nine times a virgin? Pauline was a bright girl, was she a professional virgin? My gut tells me all the engagements ended after a brief time because Polly, deep down, was an agile, respectable, convent-raised Catholic girl. Pauline wanted exactly what she desired before finally being unbuttoned from those pink pajamas.

Great expectations were being heralded in all the newspapers about the 1910 Christmas voyage. The attention centered on the much-ballyhooed attempt to break the world record for the round-trip from Liverpool to New York and home again. We even had a reporter from London's *Daily Mail* traveling with us as a special correspondent for the trip, hell-bent to set his own record.

Homeward: New York to Liverpool, Day V

Epicurus was touring with us on this crossing of 22 December 1910. The swift Cunard liner was steaming toward Liverpool on the last leg and final night of the round-trip journey. In her hold were over a thousand tons of Christmas packages and four thousand sacks of holiday mail. Without fail, concealed among the 1,800 passengers, we were able to conscript fresh novitiates. Fresh to the table were Alexander Montgomery (AM) and Edith Wooster (PERA) Carlisle. Edith, a San Francisco–bred lady, found her way to marry the cheerful Irishman. Harriet Blanche Lawrence (BRIGHT EYES), an actress who flattered our table, was praised as the *Philadelphia Star* of vaudeville (she wrote her address as 11 Rue Scribe, Paris?). She would be on Broadway in 1913 at the Lyric Theater in the play *Ourselves.* BRIGHT EYES was a seasoned vaudevillian that traveled many roads and venues, singing and dancing, a true soubrette of the circuit (even played at weddings, she confided). In 1908, while performing in *Blue Moon* in Georgia, she had an appendicitis attack (Dr. Jones breathed a sigh of relief—one less appendix to fret about).

SALTPETER, Mr. Peter Walker from England (eponymous with the English brewer, if memory serves) sat nearby. I was not sure why he chose the nickname. In folklore the name implied to impotence. You know English humor, since we had glamorous women at the table. We ensnared Ernest Arthur Hills (ARTHURIAN LEGS) and Irina Myburgh (VIVO) tableside. I spied that the former Chicago socialite was dressed ever so fashionably as she was seated. Mrs. Myburgh was heading home to London, where she currently resides after her marriage to British Barrister Alexander Myburgh. I wondered if Irina knew of his unduly publicized affair with Adelaide Williams in London in 1896?

Publisher George Henry Doran (DAD), sporting a finely made tuxedo joined the celebration. A frequent traveler to England, he had a publishing business and residence in London (he would kindly mention me in his biography *Chronicles of Barrabàs*). Last, but certainly not least, was Mr. William Ragg Holt (SCRIBENDUM), the correspondent from the London *Daily Mail*. His assignment was to report on the record-setting crossing with the added directive to see as much of America as he could during his layover in New York. Would the Heathens be mentioned in his story? Perhaps we should not expose our secrets.

"I never thought there was such a thing as an unsinkable ship. We build ships to float and not hit either icebergs or rocks," Alexander Carlisle, April 1912. In June 1910, Mr. Carlisle retired as chairman of the managing directors of Harland & Wolff, shipbuilders, builders of the *Titanic*, for undisclosed reasons (not too shoddy for a lad who started as a premium apprentice at sixteen). In 1889, he was made chief naval architect of the firm. Before his departure, all major decisions about the *Titanic*'s and *Olympic*'s designs had been finalized. He was responsible for interiors and safety concerns on the *Olympic*-class vessels, but his expertise was evident many places on the ship's exterior.

Suffice to say that he did argue for more lifeboats on the *Titanic*, but his brother-in-law, Lord Pirrie, chairman of Harlan & Wolff shipbuilders, disagreed, being satisfied that that ship carried 50 percent more lifeboats than required by the Board of Trade in 1912. Mr. Carlisle was able, through persistence, to get the Welin Quadrant Davits installed, to carry the lifeboats on the *Olympic* and *Titanic*. These could bear four times the number of lifeboats than the sixteen that were required by law. Bruce Ismay, chairmen and managing director of the *White Star Line*, overruled the idea of additional lifeboats for economic reasons. Mr. Ismay was extremely adept at finding one of those scarce lifeboats on the night of the disaster. Fellow Heathens Leonard Peskett and Alexander Carlisle were both under intense interrogation when the Board of Inquiry convened to examine the *Titanic* disaster. Of most consequence is the fact that Lord Pirrie, who oversaw the completion of the *Titanic* and exempted from appearing, never even provided a written statement to that board. Mr. Carlisle and Mr. Peskett were given a rousing exoneration.

Being the Irish privy councilor in the House of Lords in England is a position of prestige, requiring an appointment by King Edward. A seasoned politician, Mr. Carlisle began his political career in Ireland while in his thirties. In 1920, that assembled group was having the second reading of the Irish Coercion Bill when Mr. Carlisle stood behind the rail at the steps to the throne—yes, *the* throne; his position as privy councilor gave him that access. He proclaimed, "If you pass this bill, you may kill England, not Ireland." No reply, dead silence, and Mr. Carlisle left the house. A few days later, Earl Curzon, acting at the behest of the House of Lords, sent a demand for apology to Mr. Carlisle, who replied that if he had offended the king, he was ready to make ample apology, but if it was solely intended as an affront to the House of Lords, then the case was different. He was then disbarred from the house.

The king refused his resignation and he was reinstated. In 1921 he proposed a Committee of Thirteen to bring together the British government and Sinn Féin to resolve their issues. Never thought about seriously, that crisis escalated. Mr. Carlisle was good friends of German Kaiser Wilhelm II. Did you know the Kaiser blamed lawyers and diplomats for starting the First World War? Mr. Carlisle would become an indirect victim of the Kaiser. After visiting the exiled German Emperor in Doorn, Holland, he became ill with a severe cold, which worsened. Knowing he was dying, he prepared a Heathen ritual.

Heartbroken by the *Titanic*'s sinking and loss of life he nonetheless attended the service for those victims at St. Paul's Cathedral in 1912. Overcome with emotion at that service, he fainted during the playing of the "Dead March from Saul." Vowing not to subject any of the attendees at his final rite to a similar experience, he paid in advance for the cheerful service he desired. He stipulated, "No grieving, no hymns, no prayers, no religious service." In 1926, he reaped his money's worth. A crowning departure it would be, his coffin was carried from the chapel to Golder's Green Crematorium while the organist played the waltz from the celebrated London show *The Merry Widow*. His wife and son were fine, but one of his daughters, the Baroness Von Versen, fainted during the unusual ceremony and was carried out. She was married to the former Kaiser's longtime aide, Baron Frederick. Dr. Jones wished he had envisioned such a cheeky grand finale for himself!

I would like to add a brief description of the dining room. Our first-class saloon is a singular work of art. The walls were covered with carefully grain-matched oak, each panel uniquely handcrafted (termed the Francis Premier style—I'm personally not sure what that means). The other rooms where our beloved infidels gathered were equally elegant, but the high-galleried dining room was breathtaking, rich, and airy in feeling. Bedecked splendidly for the holiday, bountiful velvety red poinsettias centered sur la table upon starched, bright-white linen. Christmas trees decorated with Victorian ornaments stood at attention against the outside walls.

Towering above the central well was a marvelous cream and gold dome, open to the floor twenty-eight feet below, while the lower dining room extended the full eighty-seven-foot width of the ship. The octagonal clerestory was adorned with fanciful wood carvings, some depicting the signs of the zodiac. Concealed lights around the domes perimeter created the effect of the soft glow of warm sunlight against the gilded convex disk.

Two hundred skilled Palestinian woodworkers spent two years on the ship's interior, which exhibited their opulent talents. On the floor were cerise-colored (think deep red to pinkish) carpets. On the lower level, you would find the captain's table in the middle of the room. To the port was the staff captain's table, and on the starboard was the best table: the Heathens'. Additional seating was available on the second-story, upper-saloon balcony, which surrounded and overlooked the open central lower section. Dark-figured, straw-colored oak-paneled walls surrounded the outer periphery, while massive dark wooden Corinthian Greek columns with ornately carved capitals supported the upper mezzanine.

Seating was comfortable and spacious, yet a not so select few of the Heathens felt the legs of the chairs were not supportive during our ritualistic celebrations. The four ornately turned legs were stabilized by short "feet," about six inches in length. The legs were closely centered on the inner portion of the chair's seat rather than the outer, like most chairs. This could add instability and danger to a perpetually teetering Heathen during choppy seas. They would soon be replaced, the chairs. Whether the ladies were resplendent in the latest Paris fashion or the men were cloaked in white ties and tails, the first time seeing the first-class dining saloon simply takes your breath away.

The ladies felt sorry for the poor goose sitting in the middle of our table. Ultimately, by supper's end, only the corpus not so delicti remained. Soon, Mr. Holt regaled the brethren with his tale of the whirlwind US visit. Mr. Holt was a diminutive, slightly rotund man, maybe five feet two at best (my being five feet seven, I felt tall for once), but his size did not diminish his story. His goal, he stated, was to do as many things as possible in the time between his arrival 5:00 a.m. Friday morning, and sailing home, 6:00 p.m. Saturday evening, a thirty-eight-hour tour. He laughed when he described how he got off the boat early by being lowered over the side into a waiting tugboat at 3:00 a.m. by rope under his armpits. Mr. Holt was dismissed from the usual quarantine and immigration period. By then, he was a fellow tribesman. I examined him immediately after supper. Physically healthy, but nothing could be done for his post-initiation mental condition.

SCRIBENDUM's first stop was Washington, DC, to meet President Taft, House Speaker Uncle Joe Cannon, and Vice President Sherman. Next was a quick tour of the capitol, including the Smithsonian, Congress, and Navy Department. Then he was off to Philly and Baltimore, spending twenty minutes in each town *taxicabbing* (a new expression to a sailor), which authorized his ability to say "I was there." Returning to New York, he queried Sarah Bernhardt (he said her dressing room was like a hothouse filled with flowers), who sent Christmas wishes to the English people. Later was the opera house and Geraldine Farrar, who was about to take stage for the second act in *Faust*. In turn he was off to the Miner's Bowery Theater, then consuming food at the East Side and Tom Sharkey's restaurants between interviews. Let it be noted that he met the New York mayor Gaynor and New York governor Dix. Ad infinitum, but not quite ad nauseam. Maybe the goose *was* the happiest creature at the table.

Set the record we did. The ship arrived in Liverpool greeted by searchlights, flares, horns, and rockets. A chorus of sirens from the other ships in the harbor heralded our feat. The band came out on deck and played holiday songs. What a spectacle. The new round-trip record was eleven days, fourteen hours, and seven minutes. SCRIBENDUM had his story, and the crew could enjoy a well-deserved Christmas at home with their families.

Jewel thief on our ship? Impossible! On arrival in New York, Mr. Dario Del Castillo, a forty-six-year-old planter from Bogota, Colombia, was arrested. Taken before a New York magistrate, he found himself accused of heisting diamonds and emeralds owned by the Colombian government. Customs officials seized ten thousand dollars of the precious gems from him as bond until ownership could be established. He told the magistrate, "I bought these goods from a person I did not know in Magdalena in 1900."

After his New York release, Mr. Castillo booked passage on the next vessel bound for England. He chose well, at least for five days. When the *Maury* docked at Fishguard he was arrested again and imprisoned for the same charge. The date 23 January 1911 made Dario a happy man. When the Colombian government failed to send the necessary evidence to England within thirty days, the British court released him. The existing terms of the extradition treaty had been violated. I never did see Mr. Castillo again.

Homeward: New York to Liverpool, Day V

Most of the gossip of our previous misdeeds must have been swept overboard into the chilly Atlantic. The second month of 1911 found new acolytes eager to participate in our rituals, and we were continuing to attract the heretofore uninitiated. The date 5 February 1911 found a spellbinding blend of souls around our fair table. The outgoing Lallie Williams, a.k.a. Alice Francis Thurgate, renown on the vaudevillian stage as a most graceful dancer and played a role in the production of *Fix in a Fix* in 1904. The London-bred actress retired after catching the eye of and marrying Harold Williams, son of theater owner Percy G. Williams, in 1909. Harold had the grandiose idea to connect all theaters with a wireless system that bypassed phone lines to ensure secrecy. (Harold's father owned a lot of theaters) The experiment remained just that. She would later divorce Mr. Williams, citing coolness and violent temper in 1925. They were not blessed with children, which made perfect sense.

Immigrating to America in 1886 and becoming a successful lumber merchant was Salvatore D'Antoni (SALVATION MUELY), a happy Heathen. He immigrated with just a dream from Cefalù, Sicily, at twelve years old on the SS *Letimbro*. My assistant James A. Corbitt (CUPID CHERUB) joined the group; he would later become chief surgeon on the *Aquitania*. After a minimal amount of persuasion we were able to get William Holmes Hossack (BRO BILL), captain in the British Royal Naval Reserve, to the table,he would later become staff captain on the *Lusitania*. Mr. Ion Hamilton Benn (BIG BENN) and beloved English actress Lena Ashwell (QUEENIE) completed our group this evening. Mr. Benn was a freshly elected Conservative member of the British Parliament (not so conservative this evening). Applauded as England's most emotional actress, Miss Ashwell was on her way to America to star in the play *Judith Zaraine*, which was opening on Broadway for the upcoming season. The fifty chefs in the galley found the time to coordinate a sumptuous menu: Tournedoes Lallie Perdreaux a la Big Benn and Glace D'Antoni Salumley, and the highlight was the Saumon "Queenie." We were honored to have such willing, yet upstanding, inductees. The menu was signed and logged into the archive.

"Did you ring, sir?" Lena confessed the story of her stage debut in 1892 at the Grand Theater in Islington. In the play *The Pharisee*, she had one speaking part, and she walked onstage and then off, never saying her single line. Stage fright, for certain. We forgive her. Lena was found after winning first prize in a contest at an acting school, while living in Brockville, Canada, near the Thousand Islands. The contest's judge was none other than one of England's most revered actresses, Dame Ellen Terry.

Nonspeaking, walk-on roles were her bailiwick for the next few years until one afternoon, she received a telegram that read, "Miss Winfred Emery sick. Will see about your boots." At the time, Lena was understudy to Miss Emery in the play *Frau-Frau*, and the play began with her entrance in a riding habit. Lena entered, spoke her lines unflinchingly, and never had to worry about being cast as lead in a play again.

Lena found time to marry famous English actor, Arthur Playfair in 1896, but divorced him in 1908, citing "cruelty", not very fair at play was he? Let us not be too quick to judge. Arthur began divorce proceedings over her affair with actor Robert Tabor in 1903. Lena was an active leader in the anti-militant women's suffrage movement in Britain and managed the King's Highway Theater until WWI began. Her brother, the mounted Canadian policeman, adventurer, and novelist Roger Pocock (*Outrider of Empire, The Dragon Slayer, Follow the Frontier*) who was most famous for his 3600 mile "longest horse ride down the Rocky Mountains" from Canada to Mexico. Having inherited the same gusto, she organized the first large traveling theater company to go overseas during the war. Her groups put on 2,300 shows in nineteen months, three shows daily across the channel in camps throughout France, of which she often starred—that's a trouper for the troop's nonpareil. Lena said men, during war, prefer Shakespeare.

Queenie was born on a ship on the River Tyne, the TS *Wellesley*. Her father was a navy captain, who later took his holy orders and moved to Winnipeg, Canada. The ship was mostly inhabited by boys so far not convicted of a crime. For her war efforts, she was awarded the OB, Order of the British Empire, from a most grateful country.

One amusing story took place in 1912 Lena, her husband Dr. Sir Henry Simpson, the Royal Obstetrician, and playwright Anthony Hope, of the novel *Prisoner of Zenda* fame, were accused of slander and brought into court. They were accused of smuggling twenty-eight bottles of champagne into their box at the Three Arts Club's Masquerade Ball, a charity event in London town. Mayor G S. Elliot,proprietor of the theater, felt he was being cheated of his profits since all liquor must be purchased from him. Confronting Mr. Hope with a hamper he asked what was in it, who answered that, "there were some provisions". In the ensuing conversation Elliot claimed he "had just done the same thing to Lena Ashwell". After Queenies testimony she blushingly admitted she "knew little of the law and had never been arrested before". The judge awarded Mr. Elliot, the plaintiff, what he thought was more than adequate compensation, a single farthing (a quarter penny). Queenie had chosen her nom de tribe wisely as her husband would, in April, 1926, bring forth baby Elizabeth to the Royal Household, who would become Queen Elizabeth II. God bless our beloved Lady Lena Ashwell.

Don't worry too much about submarines, the Navy will
give them as much as they want.
—British Vice Admiral Bacon, 18 February 1918

My own Motor Launch had her bow blown off, the whole
stem with anchor and chain
and we did not get back to Dunkirk until noon the
next day.
Fortunately the forward bulkhead held.
—Navel Action off Ostend, Capt. Hamilton Benn

My tale would be remiss without mentioning more about our guest Mr. Ion Benn. As well as being a first baronet of the British Empire and sitting MP, he was a businessman and distinguished yachtsman. He won races, most famously the Dover-Heligoland Race on his yawl *Betty*. During WWI, his four-hundred-ton steam yacht *Greta* was used as a patrol boat for the English coastal waters. The ragtag fleet of boats were nicknamed the Dover Patrol and deemed despised motor launches by the regular navy. Captain Benn commanded those motor launches. He was brevetted rank of lieutenant commander and was instrumental to the Zeebrugge Raid, on 23 April 1918, and both the First and Second Ostend Raids, for which he was awarded the DSO from Britain and the Croix de Guerre from France.

These were important military targets because they were depots that harbored and supplied the German U-boats with munitions that were used to sink Allied shipping. Those very same despised motor launches risked all perils and went to rescue the navy sailors whose boats were sunk during the Ostend Raids, and brought all of them out to safety, except those killed by gunfire. I think Ion heard how one U-boat tried to sink us and was eager to make amends for the indignity directed at our sacred order. We Brits love our sailors, perhaps an inherited characteristic that derives from being born on a big island.

Bro Bill, William Hossack, RD RNR, captained various ships in the Cunard fleet, among them the *Laconia*, *Caronia*, *Berengaria*, *Saxonia*, and the soon-to-be ill-fated *Lusitania*. One noteworthy story comes to mind about Captain Hossack. In April 1916, while commanding the armed merchant vessel *Ansonia*, his observers sighted a German U-boat approaching their ship on the surface. Bro Bill slowed the *Ansonia* and brought her stern to bear toward the submarine, revealing a big six-inch gun prepared to fire. Seeing they were about to be shelled, the Germans turned tail and sped southward. They had spotted an unarmed British tramp steamer nearby and proceeded to sink that vessel, which was witnessed by the passengers and crew of the *Ansonia*. The headline reported "GERMAN SUB SCARED AWAY BY SIX GUN," which really should have said "SUB RETREATS FROM ARMED SHIP TO SINK UNARMED SHIP."

The ocean can play tricks with your mind if you stare into the vast emptiness of the horizon long enough. Passengers on the *Saxonia* in June 1921 claimed to witness a baffling vision while the ship was battling icebergs for two days off the coast of Newfoundland under the guidance of our Bro Billy. Fifteen bergs were sighted, some a half mile long, and rose a hundred feet into the sky, making progress exceedingly slow. One berg uncommonly resembled a village, including houses, churches complete with spires, and roadways fashioned in the ice. Methinks not enough ice in their beverages.

Homeward: New York to Liverpool, Day IV and V

The 25 February 1911 recruitment was singular. Adamson Parkyn, Eric McKay Reid, and James A. Pitts (MORMON GAYLE) were joined by Suzanne Jackson and Marie d'Augustynovies, or Duchess d'Olivares (SISTER DUCHESS). Mr. Pitts worked for the Atlantic Steel Casting Co. Ernest Kent (GARDEN) was a manufacturer, and Alexander Howard was a lumber merchant, both from England. Of all the guests ever received table side, Ernest has experienced most of the world. D. Adamson Parkyn was an English metallurgical engineer, not train, who built boilers for them, the famous "Manchester Boilers" at the Newton Moor Iron Works. His grandfather was Daniel Adamson, and our Mr. Parkyn's father married Daniel's daughter Lavinia in 1873.

Despair not, we had flashes of brightness. Doris Field (CHRISTIANA, Doris's daughter) was traveling with her sister, Sybil, who chose not to attend. Helen Herzberg Kaufman (SISTER) brought a lively wit to the table as well as being very pleasing to the eyes. Helen was the wife of the famous author and editor, Herbert Kaufman, who was recently signed as Sunday columnist for the *Chicago Tribune* (he was elsewhere on the ship this evening). The former Baltimore beauty, whom Herbert steadfastly wooed in college while attending Johns Hopkins, regaled the assembled with tales of their recent travels. Albert Lund, transatlantic shipper and representing Belgian shipping concerns in America, was heading home to London. Marie (with the long name) was really Angie Holman, married to Charles, and invited for her creativity in names.

Spears of Deliverance was the title of the book Captain Eric Reid would pen in 1921. The romance novel was about white men and brown women in Siam. Currently he was editor of the English-language weekly *Siam Observer*, where the future king of Siam, Prince Vajiravudh, wrote under a pseudonym. Mr. Reid had been British vice-consul in Bangkok. Prior to that position, he had war service on the Indian border and German East Africa. After hearing a few indelicate stories from him, I fancy his own life story would be a far better tale than his future novel. Cagey he must be on applying his blue pencil to tweak the prince's columns.

The headliner of this night was Suzanne Jackson (RUBY), a Montreal Canadian who was a rising star in the theater. Currently a leading lady in off-Broadway productions, traveling relentlessly to US and Canadian engagements, and being interspersed with London productions kept Miss Jackson a busy lady. She would have a long career on the Broadway stage and be instrumental in the Canadian war relief efforts.

I did not have the heart to tell Suzanne this eve that, in 1913, she would become ill from a ruptured appendix. Dr. Sydney Jones is beset from all quarters by that gland. Her condition would become critical, but not fatal, during a performance of the hit play *Because She Loved Him*. She was a "bright luminary," lifted from a critic's review I pilfered. Perchance I read too much. Suzanne's quote of the night was as follows: "Many actresses see an opportunity without seizing it. Ambition is an excuse for acting, but talent is the justification." She did make headlines for a scene in the wartime play *Seven Days Leave* in 1918. One critic wrote that she leapt naked into the English Channel sans skirt. The scene was so well staged that most who witnessed the event believed she really was naked. Those girls educated at the Sacred Heart Convent had amazing splash.

In March a brutish storm bore down on us. Eighty-foot waves smashed the wheelhouse, shattering windows several places on the *Maury*. The decks were strewn with wreckage. A railing was mangled, and parts went into the ocean. The tremendous rollers caused enough damage to delay our next departure for twelve hours.

Did I ever tell you my remedy for seasickness? I daresay my ideas were even published in a British medical journal. It is 99 percent successful. Seasickness is caused by acidosis and acetonemia when the human body is in an acidic state. Prevention is just as easy as a cure. I recommend that before sailing, the future ocean traveler should live a quiet and decent life one week before boarding ship. Avoid all bon voyage parties. Taking a simple vegetable cathartic a week before sailing is recommended. The prospective traveler should avoid beef, liver, sweetbreads, vinegar, and salt. Wines, beers, and coffee should be eliminated. However, mild cocktails of gin and orange juice or weak whiskey and water will do no harm. Remember, alcohol causes an unfavorable reaction when the ship moves. If it doesn't move, alcohol is permitted.

If you are unaware of these precautions, I have a simple elixir. All genuine cases of that loathsome malady respond to intensive alkaline treatment. Citrate of soda works on most patients. Depending on stomach conditions, I add a bit of bromide or a small quantity of strychnine for tonic. Sometimes, citrate of bismuth is combined with a tonic. We did attempt to time our initiations with the dinner d'adieu (farewell dinner), while anchored overnight in quarantine, but that sorcery floundered often. This remedy will likewise work for air sickness. Heathen physician, heed thine own remedy.

The High Priestess lost her white Boston bulldog, King, near Times Square in April 1911.How one endowed such otherworldly powers can lose a dog is baffling. After placing a Lost and Found ad in the *New York Times*, offering a liberal reward, the dog was returned the next day. Constance divined a peculiar time to lose her beloved pet during the middle of the short run of her current play *Thais* (only thirty-one Broadway performances). In her defense, the show went on a US and Canadian tour, eventually produced by Sir Tree in London. Perhaps the powers of the High Priestess extracted a little more magic from May Blayney's gift of a white elephant.

Homeward: New York to Liverpool, Day V

May started as February departed, too few stalwart soulless people possessing the true bohemian brio for adventure. Potential members were in scarce in supply, maybe fearing more big waves would be conjured forth if they dined at our table. The May 7 version was unremarkable, except for the presence of actress Irene Fenwick (FRIZZIE), the future Mrs. Lionel Barrymore, fresh off her performance in *The Zebra* (which is a balloon) at the Garrick Theater in New York. Irene did me the great courtesy of not having her appendicitis on any of my ships. Mary Letcher (SISTER MARY) and I were the only other two attending. Mary, being a fellow doctor from Richmond, Virginia, made our conversation about annoying organs stimulating.

Irene was heading to England, where she would soon introduce fellow Heathen Pauline Chase to Mr. Robert Goelet, one of the richest, recently divorced young men in New York, at a banquet at the Carlton Hotel. The next day, Miss Chase acknowledged her disengagement to Claude Grahame-White, keeping her established tradition intact. Pauline was fortunate to make her relationship with Mr. Goelet brief. He soon married a different young woman, and the marriage lasted a few short years. Court depositions disclosed that he treated his wife with inhumane cruelty.

Outbound: Liverpool to New York, Day V

18 May, 1911, breathed new life into our mission. A cadre of novitiates surrounded the table. Amy and Edward Hoblyn, Frank Roberts, Ernest Kent, Robert Deford, Alexander Howard, Salvatore D'Antoni (one of the brethren returned), and Muriel Elfreda Barneson were administered the oath and downed the obligatory libations. The Hoblyns were an enjoyable and well-traveled couple. He was employed as a passenger agent for the Cunard Lines. Frank Roberts was a wheelwright; a change of occupation from what we were accustomed. Alexander Howard was in the lumber business. Canadian ship owner Robert Deford endorsed Canadian schools, he had recently donated fifty thousand dollars to McGill University; he could afford that amount. Ernest Kent (GARDEN) of England manufactured things, which he never divulged. When signing his departure papers I took a peek at his occupation; just as he asserted.

Muriel Barneson, the prominent San Francisco socialite, was a temporary London resident. She was active in the American Women's Club, which engages female expatriates in social, cultural, and philosophical endeavor (meaning she had too much money and time). She had recently completed six months of music studies in Paris. She was the daughter of the famous Captain John Barneson, a wealthy ship owner and oil magnate of San Francisco. In 1919, he would sail his 135-feet schooner/yacht *Invader* twenty thousand miles around the world. Muriel often joined him on his journeys, habitually aboard for the last leg of the journey. Now this *Briny Marlin* American gal had a pair of well-seasoned young British sea legs.

Homeward: New York to Liverpool, Day I

The last party in May on the twenty-eighth was again short on novitiates. All the potions I had mixed as offerings to the sea gods to incite them to look more favorably upon our enlistment had gone unanswered. We did manage to amass three and they were bold enough to choose nicknames: actress Miss Ida Barnard (EVE, her mark the apple), Myra Seymour (MOTHER), and of singular note, Pablo Escandon (GOV). Ida was recently in *Marriage a la Carte* at the Casino Theater on Broadway. She traveled the United States and Europe extensively and would become a frequent guest at the Heathens' table.

MOTHER was the mother of an enticing daughter, named Merelina, and son, Gordon. Her deceased husband was British General Frederick H. Seymour, owner of the Torres & Prietas Railroad in Mexico and estates in Torres, Mexico, and Redondo Beach, California. Mother and daughter were skilled tennis players and golfers, Myra playing in golf tournaments across America. Most curious to the Big Chief was that Myra's daughter, Merelina, had met her future husband, Asbel Newel, superintendent of Mexican National Railways, at the home of then-president Diaz in Mexico. Our fellow traveler, Mr. Escandon, was on President Diaz's staff at the time and here we found them together on the *Maury*. MOTHER and GOV, my mind was bemused and still remains thus.

Those who followed the polo competitions knew Mr. Escandon as a member of the bronze medal–winning Mexican polo team in the 1900 Olympics. In 1903, he gained notoriety for grabbing the gun away from a would-be assassin of then–Mexican president Diaz while acting in the capacity as his chief of staff. The coronation of King George V in June was Colonel Escandon's reason for this voyage and he was heading the Mexican delegation to my country. The very wealthy landowner and successful horse breeder was, in 1909, elected governor of Morales, Mexico.

The tales told about him were as plentiful as he was colorful. I will just convey the facts, not the gossip. He was arrested and sent to the penitentiary for voluntarily aiding and abetting the revolutionary Zapata, but was released for lack of evidence.

In the near future his sugar crop was burned, resulting in a million-peso loss, including his three haciendas, by those same Zapatistas he was accused of aiding. In March, he was chasing the Zapata rebels and cornered 700 of them in Jojutla, Mexico, but sent for reinforcements without firing a shot, the rebels disappeared during the night.

In November 1912, he would be arrested again for giving money to the rebels. As before, he would be released for lack of evidence (bribery will set you free in Mexico). This plucky chap knew how to play for both teams on the polo field, and it appears survival in Mexico during those turbulent times required those skills. That dexterity expired for him in October 1917 as he, and twenty-two others, were arrested and summarily deported from Mexico for conspiracy against the newly elected Carranza government. He would later seek asylum and eventually reside with his family in Laredo, Texas.

His masterful finesse did not pass on to his son. One day, at the Mexican Jockey Club, Pablo Jr. shot and killed Maderista leader Manuel D. Asunsulo over a political dispute. When Pablo unholstered his gun, it discharged, shooting himself in the leg, yet still managed to shoot his outspoken rival. The shot severed his artery, and he died shortly after the leg was amputated. Poor Pablo Sr. had a sad day coming down the el camino. On a more cheerful note, the Mexican delegation was bivouacking at the first-class Hyde Park Hotel, London. The Gov was a charming Heathen and a quite likable fellow.

My posthumous meanderings might seem to have become banal. Forgive the long-forgotten old surgeon for seizing this long minute for one last grasp at a thread of mortality. The dusty box of darkness within which our archive has dwelt for these last one hundred years has that effect.

Why am I waxing melancholic? Please permit me the indulgence of relating how someone so beloved and famous can be almost completely forgotten by history. I am speaking of our most adored passenger and always loyal Little Mother, Alice Lloyd. This petite little lady could fill a music hall to capacity night after night, year after year. She crisscrossed America from coast to coast and the ocean for two decades. Audiences adored her, so much so that she was the highest-paid actress in the country, earning $2,500 per week (the royal suite on our ship cost $2,450 for five nights; to have known Alice was worth more). Tirelessly, she sang, danced, and acted on practically every important stage in the USA, Canada, Australia, England, and even South Africa. One thing this old sea dog can do is peer into your mind. Alice who? Well, for the first quarter of a century of the last one, everyone knew that name, which brings us to our next consecration.

One thing that must have become fairly obvious by this pint (oops, I lost an *o*—I meant *point*) is the fact that the flock was much more epicurean than nefarious. Dining, drinking, and laughing were really our only secret. Membership was open to anyone with those same inclinations. The night of 15 June 1911 began a three-day party, and I, for one, was thankful when the ship reached quarantine in our home port of Fishguard.

Homeward: New York to Liverpool, Days I and II and?

As with all new Heathens, I will leave it up to the reader to determine their net worth to society. Tribal troupe accounted for were Tom McNaughton (PHUNNY PHUNSTER); Alice Lloyd (LITTLE MOTHER); Fred W. Popple (POPPY POP), our resident globe-trotter, banker, and occasional horticulturist; and Alexander Howard. New initiates were Elalia Gray (ANTIPON), Ernest Kent (GARDEN), Robert B. Smith (JEFF), Mark Leuscher (MUTT JR), and Chauncey McCormick (THE LODGER).

A very enticing and shapely housewife, Mrs. Gray's choice of ANTIPON might need explanation. First appearing on chemists' shelves in England in 1904, the pleasantly citric bottled liquid was a remedy for all that ailed you. Curiously, the product was a cure for corpulence (three pounds per day could be lost) as well as for restoration of beauty. Elalia was living testimony to either its wondrous effect or, from my perspective, its complete lack of necessity. The ubiquitous restorative would outlive me. This was the warm-up night. Behavior was modestly cheeky.

Unholy Neptune . . . or not. The day 16 June 1911, I lost control of the sacred scrolls. The gourmands decided to enact new rituals. I did manage to get the menu signed by those within reach, which I will list by their meal names.

Caviar (favorite fruit of the Oom Cum Tribe)
Cantaloup de Lodger
Petite Marmite Little Mother

Troute Sister Troutman
Spring (Maid) Lamb McNaughton
Asparagus Leuscher
Salads from Bro Kents Garden
Peaches a la Alice Lloyd
Champagne Popity Pop Popple
Cheese and Crackers Bro Howard
Coffee Sister Antipon
Liqueurs and Cigars Robert B. Smith Brand
Birthday of Alice Lloyd (sweet seventeen)

Emily De Birmingham (SISTER BIRMY) and Bessie McNaughton (SISTER BETTY) did not get a dish named after them, but they were quite the dishes all the same.

First act of business was to introduce the investitures. Hazel Troutman (Sister Trouty) was a young actress who had just finished ninety-six performances in the *La Belle Paree* at the Winter Garden Theater in New York. She would soon be appearing in the huge hit *The Girl from Montmartre*, along with fellow Heathen Dai Turgeon (SISTER SUNNY). Her first big hit was *45 Minutes to Broadway* in 1907. During a foggy spell, I happened to find a rather nice picture of Hazel and Prince Brancaccio of the eponymous olive oil importers at the New York Horse Show at Madison Square Garden in 1912.

Reputedly a man had died attempting to light the prince's cigar. A wee bit of detective work ascertained it to be true. A mail train guard had repeatedly tried to light a match while standing on the outside of a rail car traveling from Rome to Naples in Italy in 1888. Obstinately insistent upon fulfilling the task, he was heedless to the narrow bridge and its approaching railings. He was crushed. Prince Brancaccio fainted. Later, the widow received $2,000 from the Prince. Herein must be a lesson.

Marc Leuscher (Mutt Jr.), the recognized snazzy dresser and Broadway producer, was currently producing a hugely successful Broadway operetta named *The Spring Maid*, starring one of our own, Tom McNaughton. (Was this the night when Phunster became a silent partner with Mr. Leuscher?) Mr. Leuscher's aspiration this crossing was to secure a suitable play for famed actress Lillian Russell in London.

Robert B. Smith (Jeff), lyricist, songwriter, and author, had the privilege of writing the music, along with his brother, Harry B. Smith, for the previously mentioned production. They were all on intermission from the show, while the production was being moved to a different theater. A brief vacation in England was in order. Bessie McNaughton was Tom's dear sister and Emily De Birmingham was the wife of Dr. Jose De Birmingham of New York. Emily, seemingly, was accident-prone. A negligent motorist in Washington, DC, had left a splashboard on the sidewalk and she tripped over it, breaking a wrist, necessitating three weeks of recovery in Georgetown Hospital. Dr. Jones would not tolerate a patient lounging that long in his sick bay over such a minor injury. Much to the dismay of the owner of the offending fender, she did obtain a cash award for $2,500. Please stay away from the ship's railing, Emily.

Elizabeth "Bessie" McNaughton was a tall, thin, attractive, aspiring actress, who could possibly have been imagined as a murderer's accomplice in an international manhunt. She was married to Phunster's brother and former stage partner, Charles. Passengers on the *Majestic* were convinced she was the notorious woman as they followed her around the ship for days, comparing her to pictures of the notorious Ethel. When the infamous Dr. Crippen killed his wife, Belle Elmore, on 31 January 1910 and then fled England with his mistress, Ethel Le Neve (she was disguised as a boy with easily observable curves) on the SS *Montrose*, Sister Betty was unconcerned.

On the morning of 23 November 1910, the homeopathic, homicidal Dr. Crippen was hung, and that very same morning, Ethel planned to resettle in the United States. A telegram was sent to immigration authorities in the United States, claiming that she was en route on the *Majestic* under the name Miss Allen. Believing Bessie was Ethel she was detained at the pier and persistently questioned by the immigration authorities. Her sister-in-law Alice Lloyd had sent her agent, Pat Casey, to meet Bessie but was late because of a chauffeurs' strike in New York. When he arrived at the quay, he was able to resolve the situation with the officials, and she was released into his custody, her ordeal at an end.

The same trip had dockside drama before the *Majestic* departed Cherbourg, France. Fitzgerald, a water tender on the ship, was stabbed to death by a dockhand. Seconds later, a sailor fell from the ship and drowned, all happening while passengers were lined along the railing, waiting to depart. Sister Bessie, now of the clan Heathen, should have no further problems traveling, and hopefully less commotion.

Always ride in a taxi, so one will not run you over.
—Mark Leuscher

In 1906, the aerial garden rooftop theater opened with Fay Templeton as the headliner. Business was slow as the elevator was daunting to would-be patrons. Each night, the actress received a mash note and gift from an admirer named Thomas Lanphier, which she returned, and was dutifully reported each day in the papers by Mr. Leuscher. One day, the papers printed a photo of Miss Templeton holding the last letter written to her, proclaiming a broken heart and undying love and a man's hat with the letters *T. L.* on it. Mutt Jr. wrote in the paper that Thomas had committed suicide. Needless to say, the show played to capacity crowds for months. Guilt-ridden, the young actress later confessed the ill played shenanigans were a publicity trick. The passionate verse had been written by Mr. Marc Klaw, the theater owner. Mr. Leuscher, unquestionably, had the exclusive story, culpability, and byline.

Now ready for Broadway, Mark teamed with Louis Werba, whose first play, *The Deacon and the Lady*, only ran for sixteen shows in 1910. They would produce *Little Miss Fix-It* in 1911, starring Nora Bayes, with four times the longevity of *Deacon*, but was not enough to pay the bills. Alice Lloyd would take the same show on a long road tour to much-better success later in the year (it would lead to her being the only vaudeville star to grace the cover of the prestigious *Theater Magazine*). Several other plays followed in quick succession. Their collaboration would last until 1914, when they found themselves bankrupt, along with fellow Heathen Tom McNaughton. Mark moved to a farm in Connecticut and raised dogs for five years, Airedales. Gone but not forgotten, he accepted an offer to become general manager of the Hippodrome in NYC, the largest theater in the world. In 1917, he would win the handsomest man in New York contest sponsored by the *Evening Mail*. Later working for RKO, he was always the man about town and known as the "go-to guy" in NYC.

La Domino Rouge . . . was way before your time. On 18 September 1905, Mr. Leuscher had the great fortune of marrying a young dancer from Detroit named Daisy Peterkin at Notre Dame Cathedral in Paris on her twenty-first birthday. By now, the noted danseuse had *frenchified* her name to Mlle. Dazie. The play was the pivotal role and path to success for the talented and lithesome pantomime artist. She became exceedingly adored and a crowd favorite in America and abroad.

An incident in 1909 nearly ended her life. "Used wrong dirk on Mlle. Dazie" expressed the headline. Onstage during a pantomime skit at Rockaway Park Theater entitled *La Amour d'Artiste*, a misfortunate mishap occurred. During the altercation scene, actress Mlle. Lina picked up the steel dagger instead of the leather one. She was supposed to raise the genuine blade, drop it on the stage so the audience could hear the real blade clang, then stoop to pick up the fake leather one for the stabbing. Mlle. Lina stabbed her. Mlle. Dazie screamed as blood spurted out of a four-inch wound to her left breast. Several women in the audience fainted during the wild excitement. Swooning, the dazed Dazie was rushed to her dressing room for attention. She survived. A local police sergeant attending the show wanted to arrest Mlle. Lina, but Mlle. Dazie refused to press charges, claiming it to be an unavoidable accident. A year later, she divorced Mr. Leuscher, he afterward reaped great praise for the prized daisies he grew on his farm.

On this night, several pages were recorded, and not by my hand. The "Old Heathen Soake Song" was inscribed on the pages of the sacred scroll by the Phunny Phunster. Tom McNaughton might be the "funniest comedienne our stage has ever borrowed from London" proclaimed the *Washington Post.* To me he was always "phunny," but the song was definitely a drinking song paying homage to our favorite pastime: drinking. Most noteworthy this night was our first resolution as a group. Robert B. Smith was adopted poet laureate of the Grand Order of Heathens for his putting the words to music (of sorts), with a unanimous *sinkit* by those present.

Our newly enshrined laureate Jeff's first order of business was a composition, which he called "Ye Order of the Yellow Ribbon." The history of the yellow ribbon is for remembering a loved one, which goes back hundreds of years into the history of the British Empire. Our resident songster put words to music on our pages, adding a yellow-colored illumination of the ribbon.

Round her neck she wore a yellow ribbon,
Wore it in the summertime and in the month of May,
And when they asked her why the —— she wore it,
She wore it for her lover who was fur, fur away
Fur away, fur away, fur away, fur away.

She wore it for her lover who was fur, fur away,
Fur away, fur away, fur away, fur away.
She wore it for her lover who was fur, fur away.

Robert was one of the most influential lyricists of the day, and he took a most circuitous route to get there, unlike his highly acclaimed librettist older brother, Harry B. After college, he worked as a clerk for the Nassau RR in Brooklyn, New York, then under the leadership of Tom L. Johnson, future mayor of Cleveland, Ohio. During this time, he wrote plays for amateur societies and articles for the *New York Sun* and *Brooklyn Eagle* papers. Along the way he became press agent for the New York Casino and Olga Nethersole while she starred in the controversial play *Sapho*.

In 1901 he produced his first satire, *A Casino Boy*, which introduced future star Anna Laughlin to Broadway (the first Dorothy in the *Wizard of Oz*). His first hit song, "Come Down, Ma Evening Moon," was sung by the great artiste Lillian Russell. It would be a long and illustrious career. In May 1913, he married the star of the traveling production of his most prominently applauded play, *A Spring Maid*, Miss Marguerite Wright. She would retire after the completion of that tour. We were honored by his contribution, and thankfully, he asked not for payment. Who would be the first to receive the yellow neck ribbon?

One particular participant of the horde in progress is worthy of a Pivvy mention. A very young Mr. Chauncey McCormick, fresh from the coronation of George V in England, was heading back to America on this crossing. Our Lodger was a true romantic in his courtship of Miss Marion Deering. When his future father-in-law uncovered his daughter's intent to marry Mr. McCormick, Mr. Deering hastened maid Marion abroad from Chicago. His words were that Chauncey did not take life seriously and engaged in too many social functions. Lodger was gossiped to be quite the ladies' man. Not so easily dissuaded, Chauncey followed her to Paris. With unwavering persistence, he pursued Marion and her father across Europe, to Egypt, to Spain, around the Mediterranean, wooing her in person at every opportunity. What Heathen fun! Returning to Paris, Marion became of age and married Mr. McCormick in a small, quiet ceremony. Reportedly her father waived his objections.

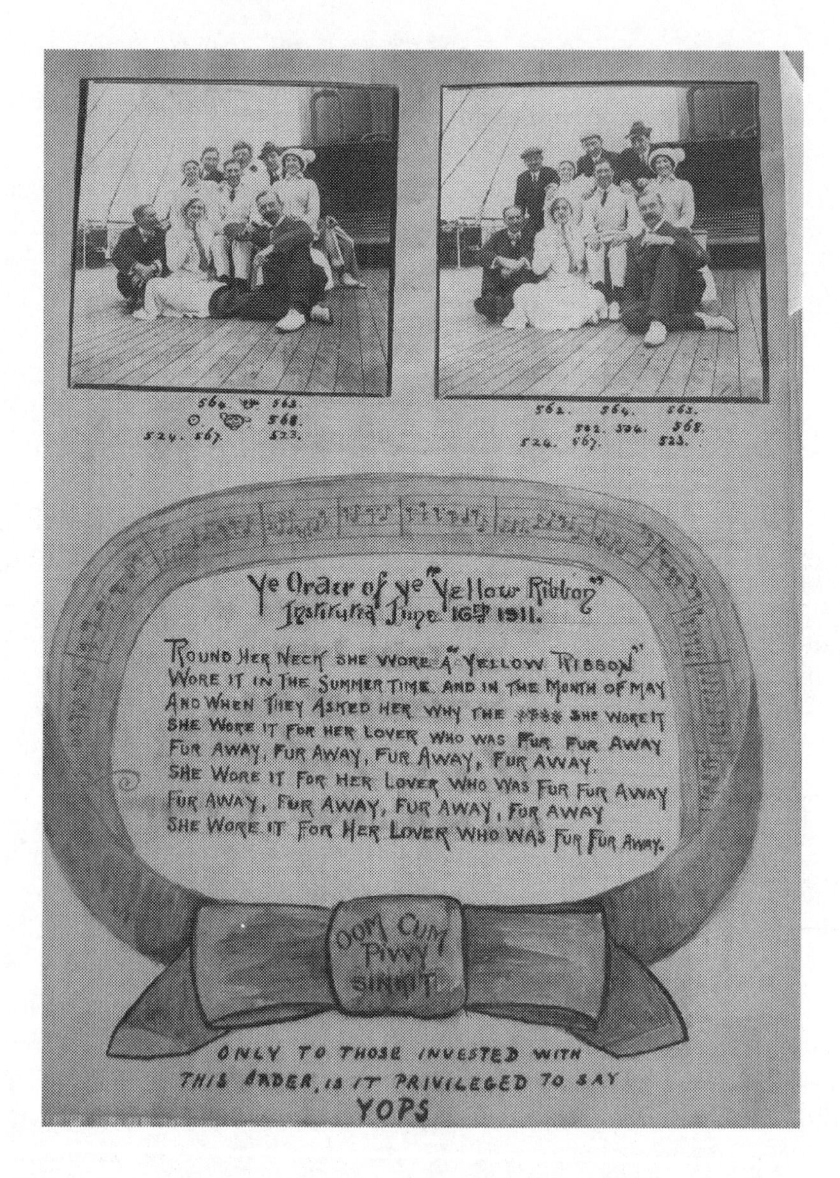

Left pic, top left to right: "Mark Leuscher" Dr B Jones" "Robert B Smith"
Middle: "Alice Lloyd" "Tom McNaughton" "Bessie McNaughton"
"Alexander Howard" "Hazel Troutman" "A E Popple"
Right picture, top left to right: "Ernest Kent"
"Mark Leuscher" "Robert B Smith"
Middle: "Alice Lloyd" "Tom McNaughton" "Bessie McNaughton"
Bottom: "Alexander Howard" "Hazel Troutman" "A. E.Popple"

"YE OLDE HEATHEN SOAKE SONG"

UNDER NO PRETENCE WHATSOEVER MAY THE ABOVE BE GURGLED WITHOUT AN OOM CUM GARGLE ACCOMPANIMENT. THIS IS FINAL

EVERY LITTLE OOM-CUM HAS A PIVVY OF ITS OWN
EVERY LITTLE PIVVY HAS NO MEANING BY ITS LONE—
= SOME = GLUB-BLUB-GLUB-UB-UB-BUB
(Delivered Mysterioso)
BUT WITH AN ADDED SINKIT, AS FROM THE GLASS WE DRINKIT,
HEATHENS TOGETHER THINKIT
OUGHT TO GO-O-DOWN ——————

IF GARGLE LASTS, REPEAT. ——————

Little Mother her Mark 502
Big Chief 506 his mark

ILLUMINATED BY PHUNNY PHUNSTER
His MARK 504

Alice Lloyd

·Menu·

CAVIAR
Favourite Fruit of the Oom Cum Tribe
CANTALOUP (de Lodger)
PETITE MARMITE (Little Mother)
TROUTE (Sister Trousman)
SPRING ("Mad") LAMB (Tom McNaughton)
ASPARAGUS Mark A. Luescher
SALADS (from Bro. Kent's Garden)
PEACHES a l'Alice Lloyd
CHAMPAGNE (Popity pop poppie)
CHEESE AND CRACKERS
"Ow Ard," Bro. Howard
COFFEE (Sister Antipon)
LIQUEURS AND CIGARS (Robt. B. Smith Brand)

Heathen Anthem by the Pivvy Choir.
Finale

Birthday of Alice Lloyd (Sweet 17).

R.M.S. "Mauretania." June 15th, 1911.

Chauncey proved his father-in-law wrong. After his marriage, he became the director in Chicago for the American Ambulance Field Service, raising and donating substantial money for the war effort. He took his duties seriously and was assigned to the French front in June 1917 as inspector of the ambulances. In November 1917 he resigned the Red Cross as an ambulance driver and became a lieutenant in the US Army's Quartermaster's Corps. He would later lead the first armored relief train to the Polish city of Lemberg, surrounded on three sides by the German army. For his humanitarian aid efforts, he was awarded the Croix de Guerre from France. Serving during the war on the *Maury* while she was in active service as a troop transport and hospital ship, I appreciated the value of my fellow Heathen's contributions. He would have a distinguished life and made all Heathens proud to have had him at our table.

I expect to live 150 years with my system of living. Proper eating, sleeping,
and clothing make up my system. I stay in bed six hours and it is so, solid sleep
and quite enough. I never intend to retire. Work made earth a paradise for me
and I don't believe there is any paradise up above. I am better able to keep
working now than I was at 25. I only eat what I wish, that is not much,
only a handful of solids at a meal. Present day dances & the modern methods
of dressing are insane . . . temporary state of mind . . . people will soon recover.
I ascribe most of the ills to which human flesh is heir to overindulgence.
—3 August 1911, T. A. Edison, disembarking *Mauretania*
(not a Heathen, but should have been)

Edison's last words were as follows: "It is very beautiful over there."

July 22, 1911, Tom McNaughton, walked through a glass door
Sunday night at the Hotel Duval in NY City with him receiving several "gashes
about his person."
—*Variety* magazine, Sime Silverman, T. M., still on the water wagon

July 21, 1911, Flapper, Tom's daughter, Alice McNaughton, had an appendicitis.
Big Chief was happy it was not on the *Mauretania* as he would not be
appropriate operating on a fellow Heathen whose father is also
one of the founding fathers of the Heathens.

Outbound: Liverpool York To New York, Day V

Barely had I recovered my bearings from the previous month's three-day event when the August 17th gathering took place, a small, but prestigious group. George H. Doran (DAD), the eponymous publisher, was back at our table, traveling with his adorable fifteen-year-old daughter, Mary (SISTER NOBLE) Doran, to London. She was three years from her debut in 1914 and marriage in 1919 to Lieutenant Stanley Rinehart, son of medical officer Major Stanley and his wife, the famous author Mary Roberts Rinehart.

Mary and Stanley became engaged shortly after meeting at her father's publishing company as he was delivering one of his mother's manuscripts just prior to his departure to Europe for war duty. When he got to France, he asked to be transferred to the front, where his mom was a war correspondent for the *Saturday Evening Post.* In 1917, Sister Noble would be the subject of Mary Roberts Rinehart's book *Bab: A Sub-Deb*, partially based on correspondence between Mary Rinehart and the flowering Miss Mary during her years prior to and during her societal debut. Lieutenant Stanley would later work for George Doran and go on to a long career in the publishing business.

Let me acquaint you with the chief naval architect of the Cunard Line, leader of the design team of our ship and the *Lusitania*, Mr. Leonard Peskett (KILTIE) OBE. Joining Cunard in 1854 as a draftsman, his skill quickly propelled him above his peers. Mr. Peskett was an advocate of Frahm's tanks this evening, which he explained, were installed on ships to reduce the ship's tendency to roll, replacing bilge keels. (Infrequently, the conversations could be technical.) He had experimented with them on the *Laconia*, where they had reduced rolling by 60 percent, and they would be installed on his newest ship the *Aquitania*.

He, like our Mr. Carlisle, never could have imagined they would soon be providing testimony to the Board of Inquiry on the *Titanic*'s destruction. Learning much from that hearing, Mr. Peskett made sure the *Aquitania* was one of the first ships to carry enough lifeboats for passengers and crew. He brought warm and engaging personal charm, which endured after he left the table. Brother Dad was elected head inscriber, and Brother Kiltie, head contriver or, more respectfully, printer and architect. I was waxing poetic myself this night.

By now, you may have gotten the impression that all life on a Cunard liner is nothing but dispensing pills and pleasing remarkable women and purposeful gentlemen. Not so. Dr. Jones would like you to know that the operatory must always be at the ready and that my office was stocked with ample supplies for any emergency. My job was relatively easy compared to provisioning the ship's galley for each crossing.

Prime your imagination for these numbers. Stowed in cold storage are 770 boxes of assorted fresh fruits; 9,600 hundred pounds of turbot, halibut, sole, and salmon on ice; one and a half tons of ling (cod); 36 boxes of bloaters (not gutted, cold, smoked herring); 500 barrels of flour; 80 kegs of butter; 20 kegs of oysters; 60 boxes of kippers; 70,000 eggs; and 5 live turtles. As you can see, those ingredients are just for some of the meals for two thousand travelers and crew, so my few thousand pills and potions may seem less burdensome by comparison. The 5 turtles are for my magic seasickness pills.

Homeward: New York to Liverpool, Day I

The day 13 September 1911 was designated for the Novitiation. Members Big Chief and Donald Newton greeted Joseph W. and Leona L. Stern (SISTER STERNY). With finely wrought cursive, Joseph (THE LITTLE LOST CHILD) Stern decorated the page. Joseph took his Heathen name from his first phenomenally successful song, which he both wrote and published in 1894, selling two million copies—not too shabby for a former necktie salesman! His musical publishing house was famous in the trade as the House of Hits.

Morris Voss (BROTHER UPDIKE), a very prosperous lace importer with a swanky Park Avenue address, told impressive stories of his travels in quest of undergarment fabrics. It saddens me to be the bearer of bad news. A few years into the future Mr. Voss struck a seventeen-year-old Leo Chester at the entrance to Central Park with his automobile. To his credit, he took the injured man immediately to the hospital, where the man was pronounced dead from a fractured skull. Mr. Voss was charged with homicide. I never did know the outcome of the case. Determined to have been an accident, there were three boys who walked in front of the car and only one was injured. All is not entirely fun and games for the impious. It saddened me that one person had perished and someone had to bear the burden of that responsibility. Hopefully, these incidents will be rare for our brethren. On a lighter note, this was the first instance where tribal members cut just their faces from pictures and placed the disembodied heads next to their respective entries in the log, floating ghostlike on the page, similar to what we are now.

Heathen Novitiation.

September 13th 1911.

Heathens Present

Big Chief [mark] (His mark).
Donald Newton.

Novitiates.

Jos. W. Stern. 591. "The little Lost Child."

Ilona L. Stern. 592. Sister "Sterny".

Morrie Voss 593. Brother "Updike".

HEATHEN NOVITIATION

SEPT. 23rd 1911.

Heathens Present

Big Chief [mark] (His mark).

Ida B Small (Sob) 559

NOVITIATE.

David D. MacIntyre (Clan) 574

Outbound: Liverpool to New York, Day II

On 23 September 1911, Henry Sanford, Charles Butson, and George Washington Clarke were three new fledglings this evening, joining members David D. F. MacIntyre (CLAN), his mark the sword (which is the real mark of that clan), Ida Barnard (RUBY), and Big Chief. Fellow Cunard doctor D. D. MacIntyre was chief surgeon on the *Saxonia*. George was currently the lieutenant governor from Iowa (he would be reelected in 1912 and elected governor in 1912 and 1914).

Henry Sanford was a last-minute passenger who had been traveling on the *Olympic* when she was inexcusably rammed by the British warship, *Hawke*. He was the wealthy son of Samuel Sanford, dean of the Yale Music School, whose father, Henry Sanford, founded Adams Express (the source of the family's wealth). Henry Jr. started on a proper heading graduating college with a degree in electrical engineering (he once helped Tesla in a wireless experiment). He would become a major in the Quartermaster Corps during WWI with fellow Heathen Chauncey McCormick. His love life, like some of his fellow converts, would be fodder for the newspapers. Most notably in 1925, it would be the three-hundred-thousand-dollar breach of promise suit brought against him by Georgia Hopkins during his marriage to his second wife, Caroline Edgar. As usual with these events, the papers never printed the outcomes, only the headlines. Most unsatisfying was that the out-of-court settlements and the ensuing newspaper silence ruined the story's end. My present powers are to no avail for resolution to these tales. C'est la vie.

Unbeknownst to our dear actress Ida Barnard was that she would be married in 1917. There was nothing unusual in matrimony, except she would marry the Rubber Man, Clarence Williams. His skill was that he could elongate his neck and limbs at will, extending from five feet ten to six feet five right before your eyes. Currently in the limelight and popular in England, he opened the Growing and Developing Institute in London for patients. He was invited to Saint Petersburg to demonstrate his talent for the czar and his family. Maybe between the Rubber Man, Rasputin, and bloody killing of his citizens, the czar would not long survive. Clarence would not have a return engagement in Saint Petersburg. I imagined our EVE had a positively immeasurable honeymoon, from the medical perspective.

Homeward: New York to Liverpool, Day III

Ancillary enlistees were abducted in a mere four days. The previously anointed acceded to the bribe of Mr. Ernest Craig (KITTEN), who graciously invited us to dine at his table. It is unwise to refuse the invitation of a first baronet and sitting Member of Parliament. Mary Galloway (MOTHER COMFORT), a homemaker and dressmaker, was a fetching young lady who dignified our table. Her husband, not in attendance but traveling with her (watching the kids), was president of Galloway Coal Co. in Memphis, Tennessee. Mr. John Keppie (NEVES WIND) and Mr. William Herbert Lee Ewart (SAUCY KIPPER) imbibed a libation or two while circling the table. Presiding over the court were Ida Barnard (Eve) and, without fail, me, Big Chief.

Lee was the attaché to the British Embassy in Washington and was an excellent steeplechase rider, winning the amateur cup at Belmont. It was acknowledged that Saucy Kipper had/was dating Alice Roosevelt, Teddy's daughter. Sagely, Lee would be getting married to Cassandra Gassiot this coming November. He would become a CBE, commander of the British Empire, in 1920 and be appointed private secretary to the secretary of state of the Foreign Affairs during the Second World War. Later he would assume the duties of High Sheriff of Wiltshire in 1942 and would have one son and two daughters. Well, that's enough prognostication for now.

A splendid evening was enjoyed, owing in no small part to the presence of one of our new abductees: John Keppie, retired passenger manager of the Cunard Lines. Very conversant and well informed he was. Eminent artist Mr. Brock had painted his portrait in oils in recognition of his forty years of service to the company, whereas no one knew where it hung.

Sir Ernest was a lot more than a mere politician and jovial fellow. The wealthy scion of a prominent collier's family, Craig & Sons Ltd. in North Wales, was on an excursion to America chasing natural resources. His first New World conquest was the desirable and much pursued Miss Anna McKay of Pittsburg. He next traveled to the American west seeking fortune, which took the form of a mine, laden with both gold and silver. In 1898, he secured a lease for a mine in the Mogollon Hills of New Mexico and greatly increased production by using a cyanide process (when the need arises I administer that in quantity to misbehaving Heathens). The mine was named Ernestine after his daughter. Production increased, and it became one of the largest-producing mines in the Southwest United States. He alluded to the fact he may be selling the mine this trip. Kitten even wrote us a poem, as follows:

Who are the Heathens? Those who live on the heath
under
the clear and wholesome sky, as opposed to those
who pine in the lowers. Meow.

Let it be written by the Kitten.

I am glad you asked how a member of England's Parliament acquired the sobriquet Kitten. Do you remember my recounting our rescuing the crew in the lifeboat of the damaged steamer *West Point*? There was an auction for one of the surviving eight-week-old cats. Mr. Craig, who was born and would, in 1933, die at his beloved Milton home in Cheshire, England, with great generosity, bought the little pussycat for one hundred dollars at that very same charity auction. I mean, the man was from Cheshire—how could he not?

Outbound: Liverpool to New York, Day V

All Hallows Eve might have been only a week away, but powerful influences hovered over our table the night of 25 October 1911. For the first time, members outnumbered apprentices. BIG CHIEF, LITTLE CHIEF (Arthur Pearse), RED MULLET (Fred Harrison), MOUSIE (William Seamen Bainbridge), BON BON (Jessie Baskerville), MINT FRAPPE (Katie Inglis), and SANDOW (Edgar H. Fourt) were ready for whatever business of monkey our tribesmen could muster.

Edgar Fourt was a prominent attorney from Lander, Wyoming, specializing in mining law. He would soon be appointed a judge in his home state. He told us of his being admitted to practice law before the Supreme Court in Washington, DC, in 1907. Katie Inglis was a winsome London beauty. She always listed her occupation as tourist on my immigration forms, which, over the next decade, I would see Miss Inglis repeatedly as she and her sister traveled extensively. Her husband,

James, was general manager of the Great Western RR in England. Mr. Harrison was on to America, doing his own type of recruiting, new acts for his Haymarket Theater in London.

Mr. Pearse had business in Colorado. At times the roving mining lawyer made the doctor ruminate about parts of his behavior, but more on him later. Jessie Baskerville (BON BON) was our star attraction, who would regale us with the best stories. Newcomers were June Wheeler Bainbridge (OCTO), celebrating her honeymoon with our own MOUSIE, Dr. Bainbridge. James E. Williams (TEMPO) was an Englishman twenty-three years young. Ernest J. M. Nash (PACIFICO) was employed as traffic manager by the Royal Mail Steam Packet Co. to arrange service for his steamships in different ports. We were informed this trip was for establishing the New York–Bermuda run. Next year, he would be preparing his company's offices for the opening of the Panama Canal. He listed his occupation as master mariner on his immigration form, which made me curious. Downstream, I will disclose a good Halloween story about his family.

Miss Baskerville was an opera coach and counseled the best singers of our time. Universally esteemed, she had her own studio at the Metropolitan Opera House. She refused our interrogations about the identities of her clients, but did reveal that one of her singing stars had just settled a controversial divorce immediately before our sailing. Miss Lina Cavalieri had just received seventy-five thousand dollars (not bad for two years) from husband, Robert Chanler, in London, after she signed a document renouncing all future claims on his estate.

In March of this year she kept mum about the secret wedding of her client, Emma Calve, to singer Alnor Gaspari. Miss Baskerville quietly purchased steamship tickets for the couple prior to departing on their world tour honeymoon. Opera great Lillian Nordica was her most famous pupil. Bon- Bon did leave us with a great quote that applied to most of her younger pupils of how they had all "the qualities of genius, except the genius." At the bottom of the page, there was a little observation by one of our fellows.

Methinks the boat is late this voyage.

It pulls a little heavy
with the immense weight of the heathens on board.

—Sandow

Not to be outdone, Little Chief added this twaddle:

I want to be a Heathen
and with the Heathens will
go awful hot in its wigwam,
but it's cooler way in.

The professional gamblers caused a flap this crossing. The crew was watchful and aware that *sharpies* were chronically on the ship to prey upon the rich and soon-to-be less rich. Four of them were working together and managed to win a nice one-day pool, which netted them $650. One in the group did not get his share and went to the other's stateroom, where he bonked his eye. After that incident, the crew posted warnings to the passengers of their presence aboard. Cardsharps and dicers were a habitual and constant nuisance. This was posted by the "other" steamship line, but not of any consequence to anyone on that voyage.

SPECIAL NOTICE

The attention of the managers has been called to the fact that certain persons believed to be professional gamblers are in the habit of traveling to and fro on Atlantic Steamships. In bringing this to the knowledge of travelers the managers, While not wishing in the slightest degree to interfere with the freedom of action of patrons. The White Star Line desires to invite their assistance in discouraging games of chance. As being likely to afford these individuals special opportunities for taking unfair advantage of others.

Titanic Passenger List, Wednesday 10th, 1912

The name Ernest Nash kept lingering inside my head for weeks, familiar but without clear recollection. Sailors always remember tales of the high seas better than other stories. I decided to research the story to satisfy my nagging curiosity. And there I located it, in an old *Boston Post* newspaper article. In 1896, three days outbound from Boston, the schooner *Herbert Fuller* had suffered a calamity. The ship's original destination was Rosario, Argentina, carrying a load of timber and five passengers. In July, the ship wandered into Halifax Harbor, Nova Scotia, being sailed by a passenger, the third mate, and the ship's steward. Apparently, Captain Nash; his wife, Laura; and second mate Herbert Blandberg were slain—not just slain but butchered with an ax—while sleeping peacefully. Chief mate Bram and Seamen Brown were arrested and charged with the triple murders. Brown was later released. Chief mate Bram, on an alcoholic binge at the time of the butchery, was found guilty, mainly on the testimony of several witnesses. His motive was robbery (twenty-seven dollars) and attempted rape of the captain's wife (evidence portrayed a tremendous struggle in her cabin). The murdered Captain Nash, whose father was a shipbuilder, had two other brothers, who were sea captains, one named Ernest Nash. Shiver me timbers.

If the passer-by give yer
Somethin' becosre 'e's sorry
Fer yer,
wot 'arm
That's wot I arst
wot 'arm?

You have read the words just as penned in our hallowed, yet previously entombed, tome. One would think that one of the world's most pervasive playwrights, on 7 November 1911, might have been a wee bit more creative, or was there an inherent profundity the Big Chief failed to grasp? Yet that is what Charles Haddon Chambers wrote. Maybe that was an example of why several years earlier, he had forsworn further poetical works.

You might be wondering who wrote such drivel. Chamber's was one of the most famous personages of his (our) day. His preceding occupations included boundary rider, a bush ranger stalking aborigines, and then civil service. Who would have guessed he could write? Diminutive in stature, but not in charisma, the Australian's long-running plays were being staged on both sides of the Atlantic. Wherever Haddon Chambers went, *he* was news. His play *Passers-By* had just premiered on 14 September at the Criterion Theater and was a rousing success. "Wot 'arm" can there be in benefaction, if the intentions are sincere.

Never a stranger on the *Mauretania*, Mr. Chambers had made newsworthy mention in the papers in July 1908 when he was kidnapped by theater producer Charles Frohman for a return trip to America. Once Mr. Frohman had the unwitting playwright on board, he made a request for a new play for his rising star, Maud Adams. He wanted a prose version of the poetical drama on Joan of Arc. "I would like it finished by the time we reached New York." Mr. Chambers had a reputation for being lazy and found the *Maury* a fine place to write. Haddon is literally industrious when pressed, and finished the play. He would complete thirty amply attended plays and make six silent films in his three decades of popularity. I ask you, how many brave men would marry a dazzlingly exotic woman named Pepita Bobadilla, a musical comedy star, in 1920, thirty-one years his junior?

The American public does not like to be worried
. Haddon Chambers 1908

The name Nellie Melba will be recognized by opera lovers (as in Melbourne). Haddon Chambers would be most remembered for his eight-year affair with the Australian prima donna. Better than any plot from his plays is how this story unfolds. Returning from a visit to London in 1880, Chambers was traveling on a ship in the company of the Montague-Turner Opera Co. He began working in management for them after arrival in Sydney (nice name). During this time the lonely Mrs. Charles Armstrong befriended the two American opera singers Annis Montague and Charles Turner. Mrs. Armstrong would, in due course, become Nellie Melba.

Allow the Dr. Jones to veer southward with a Heathen tale. Haddon left Australia and returned to London when, one afternoon, while walking in the neighborhood of the Haymarket Theater, he happened across soon-to-be fellow initiate Herbert Beerbohm Tree, actor and theater owner. Tree requested a play. Haddon rushed home to his tiny upstairs garret, finished the four-act play, and sent it to Tree but heard nothing in reply. Finally securing an appointment with Sir Herbert, Tree failed to show. Chambers "ran Tree to ground," so to speak, and followed him to the Leicester Square Turkish Baths whereupon he read him the play alternately in the hot room and cooling room. In 1888 that very same play, *Captain Swift,* opened to triumphant success. Two Heathens interacting before they ever took the oath was without precedent. Now we digress farther to the broadly publicized scandal. Between solemn patients and invigorating passengers, I have time to flesh out the truth.

In 1896, Haddon went to read a play of his to Nellie. He grasped the great talent within her that had not yet been released. The two compatriots became close, and he became her mentor. His coaching paid off, and in 1897, Melba had "perhaps the biggest triumph of [her] career" (her words) in the role of Rosina in the *Barber of Seville*. The married Melba's relationship with Philippe, Duc d'Orleans, had recently ended with his engagement to Archduchess Maria Dorothea of Austria. Like water filling a hole, Haddon fell conveniently into the emptied space. In private, she was Nellie; in public, Madame Melba. And the two, married to other people, spent noticeable hours together.

"MELBA TO MARRY AGAIN," the headline shouted on 17 April 1900. Despite later protestations as to its veracity by Melba, it was loudly and verifiably proclaimed. Melba's husband Charles Armstrong, Texas rancher, did secure a divorce in Galveston, Texas, in April, while Melba was in Paris. Melba made statements to reporters that she would marry Haddon Chambers within the next two weeks. Even though Haddon was unswervingly married, Melba repeated on 21 April that the wedding would take place a fortnight hence. And again, on 24 April, she stated, "I have already bought a house on Great Cumberland Street in London, where I expect to be very happy as Mrs. Chambers. After London season, we will spend time on my new steam yacht. Let me repeat that Mr. Chambers is very devoted."

Was this an incident of passionate promises between two married people gone awry when one really became divorced and called the other's promise due? Could it be an impassioned woman's declarations gone unheeded from her lover? No response was forthcoming from Haddon, except a small printed denial, on 26 April, of any intention of marriage since he was "contently married" to his wife. On 1 May, from Berlin, Melba issued an emphatic dismissal of the reports: "Any further tales of this kind will be equally unfounded even if the most prominent newspapers should publish them."

The secret lies within the play *Sapho*. The shockingly controversial Clyde Fitch play was produced in January 1900. The plot gyrated around Fanny LeGrand, a very seductive woman. The notorious Fanny (Sapho) has assorted love affairs with men to whom she is not married—one in particular, Jean Gaussin. Jean has an affair with Fanny while he is engaged to another woman. Jean confesses, "When I am with you, Fanny, I cannot resist you, but I doubt if this is really love."

In the play, Jean moves to the country with Sapho but grows weary and flees home. In real life Haddon devotedly summered with Melba at Fernley, an estate in England in Marlow on the Thames, while he was married and where he would be buried in 1921.

On 24 February 1900, a newspaper story was written about the condition of Haddon Chambers who was ill in Nice, France. In a sickbed interview with a *New York World* reporter, Haddon said, "The life depicted in such a play as *Sapho* ought not to be portrayed on the stage." In the play, Gaussin loses his position in society as a result of his affair. In the end, the offended seductress, after rekindling the love and commitment for her within Jean, tells him to sleep and, exultant at her conquest, leaves to be reunited with the father of her child and former lover, Flamant. Melba had a son with husband Charles Armstrong.

In 1904, the real relationship with Haddon ended abruptly. "His infatuation lasted longer than hers, and she had a lot of trouble getting rid of him" (Percy Colson). An article in *the Times of Philadelphia* additionally stated that a very ill Haddon tried hard to get his physician's permission to go see Melba in *Traviata* last Wednesday night in Paris. *La Traviata* is about a fallen woman. Noteworthy was the fact that the end of the play *Sapho* in 1900 accurately presaged his very real end of the Melba affair in 1904. The name of Haddon's second wife was Nellie, I marveled at the simplicity. Perchance the Big Chief is becoming disoriented, too much shore leave between voyages . . . wot 'arm, that's wot I arst.

Outbound: New York to Liverpool, Day V

November was memorable because we had Sir Herbert Roberts, current member in the House of Commons, and his lovely wife, Hannah, mixing business and pleasure in the colonies. He had introduced a resolution in 1905 requiring shops selling imported sweets containing alcohol to obtain a "spirit license"—not quite the expected Heathen behavior. They dined with us on the seventeenth, along with the publisher William Preston Leech, his wife, Augusta, and Barbara MacRenzie. William was a former business manager of the *Washington Times* who left in 1902 for the same position at the *San Francisco Chronicle*. His idea in 1909, while at the Hearst Newspapers, to give as grand prize a free trip around the world by having young boy and girl contestants was inspirational and dramatically increased circulation. My contest form was rejected.

Nothing gives the Heathens more pleasure than baptizing newlyweds. Walter S. Primley and his ingenue wife, Kathleen, found a respite to take repast with us. Walter was working at the family business, Wisconsin Granite Co., and Kathleen was a talented golfer, we learned. They were on their way to Paris. In the scroll, Kathleen signed her name Primley for the very first time and duly noted that sentiment next to her name. Ah, youth. I felt it would not be wasted on these two youngsters.

Everyone was on good behavior for the last episode for the year (in a way). The first incident involved a US destroyer named the *Mayrant*, which, in the process of showing off her speed, circled the *Maury* twice while we were at full speed off Nantucket, R. I. Straightaway that was not very respectful. In December, the *Maury* snapped the anchor chain during a gale, drifted across the Mersey, and became stuck in good old Liverpool mud. The misbehaving steamship was refloated after a hard struggle with the tugboats.

While at anchor on the *Aquitania* in 1928, I happened across a most humorous article. Our Mrs. Primley received a speeding ticket. Appearing in court to protest her summons, she announced to the judge that her time was worth one thousand dollars per minute (how she arrived at that number is anyone's guess). Asked why she was speeding by the judge, she replied that she had to "hurry up" to complete her shopping trip. The judge fined her two dollars but made her wait forty minutes, thus costing her $40,002., by her reckoning.

Our little December mishap delayed service for two months. Bottom plates had been damaged, and we suffered from a twisted keel, a malady for which I had no corrective, other than dry dock. Safely berthed in port during raging January hurricanes that hit the Atlantic coast, our crew members were amused to read about the little torpedo boat *Mayrant* that had outpaced us with such disdain a few years previous. After being caught in the gale, the boat was lost at sea for several days off Cape Hatteras. Battered and bruised, the boat limped into Guantanamo Bay, Cuba. She was called a hoodoo craft because of the constant repairs. Nonetheless, *Mayrant* successfully managed to convoy ships through the Atlantic submarine zones during the war. US President F. D. R's private letter to the owners of Cunard failed to prevent our ruination. We were both scrapped in the same year, 1935, adulterated for alloy.

Homeward: New York to Liverpool, Day IV

The first night of our New Year was 17 March 1912. The ship was feeling much better after a little hull repair and minor refitting. The celebration was subdued by customary standards. We feasted with W. P. Barba, vice president of Midland Steel, and his lovable wife, Letiha; Joseph Woods; William McClelland, law professor; and John MacNeill, a miner. Performing in the Seamen's Charity Concert this evening, Mr. Wallace Hartley, delivered a stupendous violin solo, much to the delight of all those gathered to witness the event.

Outbound: Liverpool to New York, Day IV

Excitement, sybaritic behavior, and invocations to Poseidon swirled around our merry table. 27 March 1912 was perhaps the best party to date. Whatever was to be remembered by the participants was duly noted in the book. Memories lost would be attributed to a case of fugue (temporary amnesia). Subdued initially, it began with the inductions of Selwyn Goldstein, Jean M. Crippen, and Wish Wynne. Now Selwyn (WHERE) was a pleasant sort, a respectable lumber merchant on his way to Honduras by way of a lengthy US via El Paso route. Jean (DOCTOR) was a recent debutante from Buffalo, graced with great humor, who had spent a month in England. For the briefest of time we believed Jean was related to "the" Dr. Crippen, the American wife slayer who had been hung in 1910. In our defense, she had a gallows and man dangling from it as her tribal mark. Intermingled with this lot was Wish Wynne (PEPSIN HOSEY), one of England's foremost comediennes and character actresses. The youthful Miss Wynne was crossing to the colonies for a fresh American tour after debuting there in 1910. My devoted Heathen duty was to chaperone her on this voyage.

Ethel Wish Wynne always knew she wanted to be associated with the stage since she was a child. Her first appearance was at twelve years old in *Dick Wittington* at the Drury Lane Theater. Her career blossomed. She acted and played in music hall and vaudeville, in mostly comedic roles. Resourceful and versatile, she was famous for her impressions of children using a cockney accent and recounting well-known fairy tales.

She later became a wireless radio star, her voice a comfort to millions during the bombing of London in the First World War. I asked her how she got the name Wish. She answered, "As a child, I was always acting in front of my mirror at home, repeating 'I wish, I wish' until this gag became so well-worn that my family retorted by calling me Little Miss Wish."

In real life, she was married to New Zealand pianist Bernard Kitchen and had a daughter, Zoe. She was a trooper until the end. She collapsed onstage and was rushed to the hospital for the second time. Her daughter admitted that she left her sickbed to perform her radio show, and, after finishing the broadcast, collapsed for the final time. What an indomitable soul.

Heathen Log. Voyage No. 51061. After dinner:—

To [illegible] at 8 a.m. (In the Care of the Heathens)

You have been a little sketch of sunshine in our hours of downs and ups during a most [illegible] voyage

Nasal Obligato, of Gargle Castle Defeat

God keeps you [illegible] at 4 a.m.

B.G. [illegible]

[illegible]!!!

Latitude = Plenty.
Longitude = Unknown } At Sea.

Very blind my Friend [illegible].

Sand love yer both!

THE FOURTH MOVEMENT.

Get on with your knitting!!

I haven't had a drink.

5 a.m.

Big chief in absolute desperation

I'll have a water!!

Plain or Soda Big Chief?

Just water Thanks!!

(Received with much scratching and coughing)

SODA H_2O

Where?

His Mark

Heathen Maxim —

"Never get into Bed with your shoes on."

Hasta Mañana

(This is where the Doctor comes in)

"Thank you very very much for the Bitter Water — I will let you know how I feel in the morning."

CHAMPAGNE St. Roger 1900

The Cork.

Lights Out 6 a.m.

We speak Water, We hear no Evil:—

I observed a line in the paper when Wish passed in 1931, it described the revered actress best: "Hundreds of thousands of listeners had enjoyed her cockney sketches on the wireless, and the children who had listened to her inimitable bedtime stories are the poorer for her passing." God bless our Pepsin Hosey.

By inebriated hand vote, the Rehoboam is the official
tribal reliquary.

I faltered in my assignment. A few stalwart souls retired to the lounge for more revelry. Two a.m., was gone in an instant. We wrote fragments of the conversation in the sacred book, filling one page with illustrations, innuendo, and humorous repartee. She was most imaginative, obviously a trouper of the first order, and kept the crowd laughing into the wee hours. Heathen maxim for the evening was: "Never get into bed with your shoes on." At 6:00 a.m., lights-out. When Wish left the ship the next day, she favored me with a small inscribed photograph of herself, a keepsake I would view with high regard. We did have quite the tally-ho.

Similar to Alice Lloyd, Wish Wynne has been nearly forgotten by history. One cannot help but wonder why such talented and immensely cherished players could be so easily forgotten. I am talking of careers that successfully spanned decades. Wish Wynne had immediate and phenomenal success in the colonies: "Her impersonations of English characters are the highest type of art yet, and the comedy is exquisite" and "The most discussed actress in America today," as described in several different papers. The theater folk trended to snub the music hall folk in our era. One writer of the London *Globe* put it best in 1913: "There is more fine character acting in the music halls of London today than in our theaters, and there is far more definite individuality and artistic temperament." Wish's best talent was her portrayal of lower-class English women with an uncanny perfection in mimicking their mannerisms and speech, tossing into the mix her own brand of humor.

My rejuvenated condition affords me a certain vantage not favored others, yet much remains unknowable. Why do some people transcend their generations and become beloved for the ages, while others fleetingly flicker and fall into obscurity? Most are hardly remembered except by their families and even that dwindles. Time is a merciless judge without allegiances, and its reasons equally obscure. In the short term, it is left to man and his judgement, equally disloyal. I was quite fond of Pepsin Hosey and Little Mother, and I delighted in their company. I truly desire that you could have known them. Our reputation ascending, you will shortly be introduced to tribal members who were better remembered. Fate makes choices without regard to my personal feelings. On these pages I proffer my respectful sentiments.

Homeward: New York to Liverpool, Day IV

Brief idylls are necessary, even the Heathen soul needs a reprieve. On 7 April 1912, Dr. Jones entertained barrister David Watson Dyer (MAINE), James McCubbin (MAC), Ida E. Williams (PANKY), and Harold H. Nevanas (THE MARINER). Ida was the wife of prominent theater owner Percy G. Williams. Ida and Percy met in their youth and married in 1885, and both acted in the Amaranth Dramatic Society. Ida told the assembled brethren a remarkable story. While having supper at home with her family one evening, after the soup bowls were removed, she asked everyone at the table, "Who turned out the lights?" Their response was that the lights were still on. A physician was called, and rest was recommended. Ten days later Panky's vision returned.

Not long after this voyage in 1916, she would be declared incompetent. In the vitality of the moment, she did tell our table of parishioners how her husband once had a traveling medicine show. He would sell liver bags containing medicinal herbs attached to a battery during the intermissions between shows—to our great delight. When Percy died in 1923 (he was worth millions), he made sure she would be well taken care of in luxury. He left a five-million-dollar estate, and when his Ida died, their home, Pine Acres, on East Islip, Long Island, was converted into a residence for indigent and infirm members of the dramatic and vaudeville professions, for whom both Panky and Percy had great admiration. Ida lived four more years than her beloved Percy.

The Dyer's are a prominent family of shipbuilders in Belfast, Maine. David told us the story of when as a young man in 1887 he, his brother Alpheus, and Joshua Trussel were on the "caulkers stage," repairing the schooner *Lillian* at their wharf. This is when the ship's hull is suspended above the water on scaffolding. Suddenly the ship "heeled over," nearly killing the surprised men. All escaped unharmed and resolved to be more cautious in the future.

Captain Harold Honey Nevanas was the marine superintendent for Norton, Lilly, & Co., steamship agents in America. Their worldwide passenger and freight services kept our newest member in constant travel. His sister, Elsie Maude Nevanas, would marry Percy Hefford, second officer on the *Lusitania* in February, 1915. He would be the officer who first sighted the torpedo that struck the *Lucy* on 7 May of the same year. Percy was last witnessed helping survivors into a lifeboat.

On occasion, we are honored with fellow Cunard employees at our table. Tonight, we were amused by Purser James McCubbin traveling home to England. Mr. McCubbin hailed from a long line of sailors and had formerly been assigned to the RMS *Etruria*. Mac longingly told us of his farm in Golden Green, just outside London, that would soon be home after retirement, in the very near future. No more angry seas, drunken passengers, or irate chefs. He explained the art of victualing, providing provisions on a passenger liner the size of our sister ship, the *Lusitania*, where he was now chief purser. He mentioned gangplank willies. These were New York reporters who would hire small boats early in the morning to ferry them out to the big liners as they idled in quarantine overnight. When they passed inspections, the liners would travel the final eight miles to pier to unload.

Mr. McCubbin would regale these reporters in his cabin with breakfast and Cunard whiskey while he sent bellboys to round up millionaires or those involved in the latest scandals to tell their stories. Sadly, MAC would not enjoy his farm as he went down with his ship when she was torpedoed in 1915. He was last seen talking with a ship's surgeon, James McDermott, who also perished. A story we later heard among the crew was that a passenger, James Leary, asked Mac about his valuables in the safe while the *Lucy* was sinking. He replied, "Young man, when we get to port, you will get them. If we sink, you won't need them"—the English way.

It is a night of a thousand stars.

Hubbard

Whenever an English ship goes down, it is not merely a loss of life but a loss of family, because all mariners share the same risks when at sea. Oceans that bestow great contentment, abruptly, can become the cruelest mistress of all. The *Titanic* affected our entire crew in both profound and subtle ways. The words "practically unsinkable" are fraught with human hubris.

> The spirit of William.T. Stead, journalist and psychic was manifested at the closing of the 5th Pennsylvania State Spiritualists Associations convention last night. Wearing a slouch hat and stroking his long beard it manifested itself to Mercy E. Cadwallader of Chicago, Vice President of the group. She was a noted friend of the eminent author, who was lost his life in the wreck of the *Titanic.*
>
> Pittsburgh Press 25 April 1912

A novella I once read, written in 1898, entitled *Futility, or the Wreck of the Titan*, foreshadowed the event. Mr. Morgan Robertson, wrote about a ship named *Titan*. The eerily uncanny parallels to the *Titanic* are cryptic. There were nineteen watertight compartments on the *Titan*; sixteen on the *Titanic*. Both boats had compartment doors that closed automatically when water touched a float. There were twenty lifeboats on the *Titanic*, while there were twenty-four on the *Titan*, which was "unsinkable, indestructible, as she carried as few boats as would satisfy the laws." Our Mr. Carlisle would soon testify about that oversight. The speed of the collision, the number of deaths, striking the iceberg on the starboard side on an April night, and lastly, the location, both four hundred nautical miles from Newfoundland, almost portend that Mr. Robertson had dreamed the incident fourteen years before the real event occurred.

If Captain Smith had read *Futility, or the Wreck of the Titan*, perhaps he had a fleeting glimpse of the ultimate irony during his moment of powerlessness. Trying to save his sinking ship, as the sounds of "Nearer God to Thee," led by Mr. Hartley, echoed over the decks, with screaming passengers jumping into the ocean and the great ship sinking beneath his feet, did he have a last thought of the ultimate futility? Mr. Hartley had made twenty-two trips on our ship and was content, and very upset that his agent told him was being "requested" to play on the *Titanic*. He left the *Mauretania* the day previous to board the *Titanic* in Southampton. Albert Einstein once said, "Coincidence is God's way of remaining anonymous." I wondered what he thought of these particular events. April was the cruelest month this year.

Once on occasion chatting with Wallace I asked him
"What would you do
if the ship was sinking." He replied "I don't think I could
do better than play
"Oh God, Our Help In Ages Past" or "Nearer My God To
Thee" he replied.
His favorite solo was Shumanns' "Traumerei."
—Allwand Moody, cellist, *Mauretania*

Shipboard scuttlebutt suggested a new invention was being installed on our boat that could detect icebergs up to fifteen miles away. Cunard added eight lifeboats and seven life rafts and hoped they would never get their bottoms wet. The old method was crude: dipping buckets over the ship's side and hauling them back with seawater then measuring the temperature of the water. Drastic shifts in sea temp would indicate the water was cold enough for icebergs, but the old method sampled water five feet below the surface.

You can imagine the scientific mind of the Dr. B Sydney Jones being intrigued when the staff captain asked me to visit the bridge to view our new frigidometer. This was one extraordinarily futuristic device. It had two external nerve centers, one on the top of the mast and the other on the very bottom of the keel. Any change in temperature activates the alarms, which are then recalibrated by knobs on the machine until the bells stop. If the ringing continues after several adjustments, it indicates rapidly falling water temperatures and icebergs in the area. I am relieved that the ship's bucket handlers will stop raiding my operatory for thermometers.

Homeward: New York to Liverpool, Day IV

26 May 1912. It was rare when England's premier actor accepts an invitation to dine with our slightly sinful group. Wonders never cease. Mr. George Arliss (DIZZY) and his wife, Florence (BOLES), herself an accomplished actress often playing opposite her husband, dined with the infidels. George and Florence had just completed a 280-performance run of *Disraeli* at Wallack's Theater in NYC. He was so accomplished at portraying Disraeli, the nineteenth-century

British Prime Minister, that he would win an Academy Award in 1929 for his role in the American film. Mr. Arthur Whyte (BOY), general manager of the Film Import and Trading Co., was trying to get Mr. Arliss into film, unsuccessfully this evening. Mr. Whyte negotiated theater contracts and was a stockbroker. If he and George were doing any business, it was not overheard.

Outbound: Liverpool to New York, Days III, IV, V

It must have been the fifth of July, or was it the sixth? No, maybe the seventh, I recollect. In truth, it was three days of celebration. Relying on the menu, we inebriated these lost souls into the sacred order. Because they were so adorable, Miss Mary E. Kingdon (ROSE BOX), our gracious twenty-three-year-old host, and her twenty-two-year-old friend, Florence Marshall (PETTIE), two traveling companions from Cleveland, Ohio, strayed into our lair. Florence was a teacher and director of the Manhattan Trade School for Girls. Jakob Cahn (FRUGAL) devoured the Heathen fruit (caviar). He could afford it, owning a seat on the Boston Stock Exchange, and later, sell it in 1919 for one hundred thousand dollars.

England's greatest tenor, Walter Hyde (WODGIE), the famous opera singer, and his wife, Esme (LOLLIPOP), were returning to England after sixty-four performances of *Robin Hood* at New York's New Amsterdam Theater. It would be his only American adventure, I am afraid. His wife, Emma Atherden, a soprano of her own merit, was, aside from raising their two children, a prominent vocal teacher at London's Guildhall School. In my usual predictive fashion, Wodgie would appear with Queenie in her concert party "Firing Line" in 1914. "An experience I would not have missed for anything," he said.

The final inductee was one strange but definitely excellent Heathen specimen: J. Mario Korbel (SCULPUS). It may be obvious by his agnomen, Sculpus, that he was a Czech Bohemian sculptor—more Bohemian than Czech, I might add. He had completed his studies at the Academie Julian in Paris. Mario was the most absorbing soul, sporting wild hair and wild eyes, and was full of life yet to be, some of which I shall report here.

"So I say slit 'em. The higher the better" was Mario's controversial proclamation made after an interview during a meeting of the National Dressmakers Association in Chicago. He moved there after returning with us in 1913. The loud and uniquely moral majority were predictably outraged and vented against his histrionics, but his work was growing in popularity and being recognized favorably. Simply good publicity, I maintained.

Perhaps the moralists put a hex on Sculpus. In September 1915, he was cruising on his boat, the *Aphrodite*, off the coast of New Haven, Connecticut, with his friend, the concert pianist Edwin Schneider. A sudden squall (they can be very sudden, you know) capsized the craft, and Mr Korbel could not swim. Nearby in a powerboat was his good friend John McCormack, the famous opera singer, who hastened to the rescue of Korbel and Schneider. Schneider was more important to McCormack, who happened to be his favorite pianist. Mario had recently sculpted the heads of both McCormack's children, with much acclaim. All Heathens should swim. If you can manipulate the gyrations involved in the official Heathen greeting, then swimming should not be difficult.

Hilda Beyer was admired as the "most perfectly formed girl in America"—not my words, but I wish they could have been. Extensively renowned as a lovely, graceful, and artistically interpretive dancer, the eighteen-year-old had been dancing around the world with the Ruth St. Denis Company. She had just posed for the entrance statuary for the Panama exhibition and several pieces to adorn the gardens of John D. Rockefeller's country home.

Heathen Novitiation

July 5th 1912

Heathen Present

Big Chief (his mark) his mark.

Novitiates

Leather

Esme' Hyde. (Lollipop) his mark, 578

Florence Marshall. Pettie. her mark 599

Mary E. Kingdon — a fish box. Steve 600

J. Cann — Saved (Frugal). Frugal 601

Walter Hyde, Wodgie. his mark 602

Addenda July 6th

Heathens above present

Novitiate

J. Marie Vortel 603

Sculpsit

His mark

[illegible]

In 1911, our resident Pygmalion had watched her dance in a matinee show in Chicago and began to model her form from memory. She was the muse for many of his statues. Above all else, he was smitten with her beauty. While in New York for an exhibition of his works, he was fortunate enough to meet her by way of Dr. Arnold Genthe, the famous photographer, and thus began a two-year courtship. He proposed, she refused, several times. Mario persisted, and ultimately Hilda consented. She was truly his Galatea, but without the complications, and they were married in February 1917, and the metamorphosis was complete. Of note were his best men: artist Walter D. Goldbeck and Ralph Pulitzer of the Pulitzer's fame. Our Bohemian traveled in the finest company, our fellows included, no doubt.

The menu offerings named for the clan are the best part of the evening, and the above-assembled postulants found themselves immortalized on a menu.

The Heathens
Cantaloupe de Wodgie
Caviar Frugal
Crème Sculpy n Plaque
Pettie Bass
Chapon Trot
Haricots Oom Cums
Pommes Pivvy
Glace Fantasies Lollipop
Friandises Steve
Dessert Bubbles
Café Sinkit

Mary Kingdon knew how to throw a party.

Outbound: Liverpool to New York, Day V

August 15 was here before I could forget July. Big Chief and Kitten, Ernest Craig, welcomed Angelique (PAW) and her husband, Charles (LALLAPALOOSA) Holman, who were returning from a holiday abroad with their two children. John McGlie (MAGGIE) was reluctantly participating. Kitten introduced his wife, Anna E. Craig (FLORA), and daughter, Anna Ernestine (ARIZONA)—now we knew where he got the name for his silver mine in America. No monkey business tonight, Sir Kitten's family is hereabouts.

Outbound: Liverpool to New York, Day IV

One of the queerest nights ever was on October 16. Only two guests signed the scroll, both of whom were not fully in the spirit or perhaps otherworldly in their own manner. Philip Michael Faraday, London theatrical producer and author, signed the book. He was more famous for his book *Rating: Principles—Practice—Procedure* on property tax, still in use. Philip had a written a play entitled *Amasis, An Egyptian Princess* in 1910. His play *Girl in the Taxi* had opened a month earlier at the Lyric Theater in London. Little did Mr. Faraday know, it would run for 385 performances.

The identity of the young lady remained a mystery. She gave her name as Violet. On the immigration papers, the name read Violet Maud Forest. As you are aware, I am compelled by law to certify the passengers' health and sanity before they can disembark the ship. Her signature in the book read Violet Maud Tree. Was this one of the three daughters of the acknowledged English actor Sir Herbert Beerbohm Tree? The age was right, and the looks were right, and being in the company of a stage producer made sense because she was an actress. Even the *V* in Violet that she signed was unmistakably hers (her mother's name was Maud). From my perspective, the entrancing young lady deliberately acted very demure, unassuming, not overly forthcoming, yet seemingly enjoying the moment. Who was our incognito sprite? She never said, and the mystery remained.

As I am not likely to be famous enough for posterity I
write this now, partly
for my own edification and, partly, I hope, for the
amusement of others.
—*Castles in the Air*, 1926, Viola Tree

In rare cases my shipboard duties are not pleasant. It came to my attention on a crossing before Thanksgiving in late November. George Millingford of England was being deported back to his home country. He was found dead in steerage, the lowest deck on the ship, where a scattering of amenities are provided. Basic food, little privacy, unlimited noise and limited access to toilets is luxury for them. It did, however, allow immigrants to travel with very finite means. Poor George was diagnosed with TB and, by law, must be returned to his point of departure. Tragically, I could not ignore his condition and, therefore, sign his immigration papers for health reasons. Did you know one in four people have died because of TB for the last two centuries? I always am confounded by the stark contrast between the extreme wealth three decks above and the gloomy conditions below being in such close proximity yet worlds apart.

The reader most likely thought scandal would be prevalent throughout this tale. Or maybe your thoughts turned to blood sacrifice, demonic possessions, and orgiastic cabin parties. When a transgression happened, the oath of the Three Monkeys was enforced. We did have lapses in decorum. We are Heathens after all.

Outbound: Liverpool to New York

The Atlantic is November cold. The Northern Atlantic, where we journeyed, constantly retained an Arctic chill: in the summer forty-one degrees Fahrenheit. It was much warmer at our table the night of November 21. Big Chief entertained and was entertained by Juliette Martin (LACKME), Anna Taylor (KENSEY), and George Elliot Fowler (CHICKEN). Juliette dressed in the most stunningly chic French gown I had ever seen. It was soon related that she owned one of the most fashionable Parisienne boutiques. At my first meeting with Anna Taylor, I thought she was the lady I had read about who had plunged 165 feet over Horseshoe Falls in Canada in a barrel in 1901, thinking she was seemingly young, attractive, and healthy.

Later recounting my thoughts to one of my junior officers, he laughed and said Annie Taylor did the feat on her sixty-third birthday. Our Kensey was an adorable English wife and forty years junior to the other Anna Taylor. Marcel Proust adjudged me fairly well with his quote: "Leave pretty women to men with no imagination." In my defense, with the luxury of so many beautiful women, I can save my imagination for other amusements.

Homeward: New York to Liverpool, Day IV

The date 1 December 1912 brought warm blooded invitees to the table. Albert M. Lawrence, member of the stock exchange and director of the US Playing Card Co., and Sidney Lister joined the intriguing Mabel Frances Skarratt for a hail and farewell supper. Mr. Lister was the passenger manager for the Cunard Lines. Now Sydney (great name, by the way) had an unanticipated theory on the average life of a steamer. He stated that an oceangoing ship depreciated at a rate of 5 percent per year, and therefore, after twenty years, a ship is practically worthless. Depreciation was due to the fact that each succeeding ship built was constructed with the sole purpose of outclassing its predecessor. This earned an awkward Heathen yawn. Our ship outlasted his theory by eight years.

"How I blessed Sydney Lister," wrote the chief purser of the British ship *Laconia*, Mr. Charles Spedding. Mr. Lister had suggested, after the *Laconia* left port in New York during WWI, that since there were so few first-class passengers, they should immediately relocate all the lower decker's to the upper decks. To quote Purser Spedding, "Had I not moved the second-cabin people from D deck, some of them would have been killed in the explosion". On 25 February 1917, near 10:00 p.m., the *Laconia* was sunk by two torpedoes on the starboard side from a German U-boat. She sunk in twenty minutes. "Truly, God bless Mr. Lister," said Mr. Spedding. I think I will relate my small knowledge of the one-time actress Mabel Frances Power Skarratt. For those who may not have heard her story, it is true gossip-column prattle.

Mabel was a stunning and vivacious American woman—aren't they all to we Brits? By now, it must be fairly obvious, that we broadly invite the most fetching ladies on each voyage to dine at our table, and Mabel was no exception. Portraying a French model named Marie Pose in May Irwin's play *The Widow Jones* at the Bijou in New York was an indisputable guise for Miss Power in 1895. Prophetically, in 1897, in May Irwin's play *Courted Into Court*, she had the role as a lady of the Dottie Dimple Company. Bound for London that same year she landed a role as a Salvation Army girl in May Irwin's traveling production of *The Belle of New York*, becoming a roommate and good friend to the show's star, Edna May, a coquette in her own right. Mabel was soon transformed into a seductive young woman in face and figure, cheerful and carefree.

While in London, suitors zealously pursued the chorus girl with flowers, gifts, and hopeful notes, seeking her affections. The stage-door *chappies/johnnies* were plentiful in my era, exhibiting themselves as single-minded, plentiful, tenacious, and a swarming nuisance to actresses on both sides of the Atlantic. The unreturned passion of the twenty-three-year-old duke of Manchester resulted in a three-thousand-dollar bracelet for Miss Power. The young duke was adept at acquiring trifles on a "tick" or credit on the family name. The reprobate had title without money and was constantly engaged to a wealthy American. The relationship was brief when he found Mabel to be equally impecunious.

In 1901, one suitor separated himself from the pack. She married Charles Sydney Skarratt, manager of the Alhambra Theater, and they resided at the prestigious Savoy Court, Hyde Park, in London. Sydney was the wealthy son of an Australian hotelier and gold mine owner. In the near future, she and her husband made the acquaintance of Gilbert George Sackville, Earl de la Warr (yes, my American friends, that is where the word Delaware originates), and his wife, the countess, at the Cooden Beach Golf Club in England.

When Charles became suspicious of her behavior toward the earl, he confronted his wife, and she confessed to adultery. Charles sued for divorce. His wife was spending too much time at the club and without him. Love letters were produced in court between Mabel and Charles proclaiming their smoldering love for each other. On New Year's Eve 1913, Boodie (his pet name for her—an Australian marsupial, commonly termed as a rat kangaroo) moved back home with the perpetually-enraptured Charles. The coming week Charles left for Liverpool on business, and lonely Mabel wandered back to her Earl de la Warr, her New Year's resolve barely lasting a full week.

Cranbourne Court
Windsor Forest
14 July 1914
Dearest Syd. I do feel so dreadful. I wish my life would end today.
I am tired of it all and I don't really care to live any longer. You said
some time ago you would not divorce me and now you have changed.
Everytime I have ever seen D I have told you and always let you know
where I was. I have told you everything I have done for ages.
I have not gone out alone with him. Please think it all over.
I can go to Switzerland or someplace and stay there a few years.
Fondest love, Maisiy
—evidence presented at divorce trial

Her wandering ceased when the earl, while on wartime duty on a ship near the Dardanelles Islands, fell ill and soon died of pneumonia and rheumatic fever. He had recently been divorced from his third wife, the Countess de la Warr, in 1915. Heathens do not count the number of marriages, only the quality. Charles was granted his divorce in 1916, the earl being politely referred to as the co-respondent. A countersuit by Mabel, accusing her husband of an affair with Miss Hewitt, employee of the Alhambra, was dismissed. Court costs were assigned to the wife, who was in America at the time.

The story does not end there. I am a fairly good judge of character. No one has seen more faces than me, but this one fooled me entirely. I often wondered that if she had not dined at our table that evening, maybe these events would never have become a savory morsel of the Heathen legacy.

Déjà vu lurks. While taking much-needed shore leave, I delved into Mabel's past. Let us return to America in 1896 momentarily. Unrevealed to Londoners, Miss Power was, at present, married to someone else. Her charms attracted unceasing admirers. She was persuaded into matrimony by an ardent and persistent Walter Loeb.

Finding her irresistible, he proposed after her matinee performance in *My Friend from India* at the Bijou Theater in New York, hounding her for six months. The soon-to-be passionate young couple strode over to the Little Church around the Corner for a brief ceremony. Her first marriage, more like a mirage, lasted one day.

The fervent beau was a dashing young man who worked as his father's secretary for the family's New York firm. His outraged father threatened to disinherit the newlywed boy when he found out. He told his plight to his new wife, "If I don't give you up, my father will cast me off, and if he does, we will starve." That is how you can only be married for a day, as the boy had no money of his own. Walter transformed into a most reasonable lad since the one-night honeymoon was over. His father arranged an annulment in 1900 (maybe not until 1906). In 1897, Mrs. Loeb's mother was appointed her legal guardian to sue the distraught lad for divorce. Shortly afterward, Mabel was in the production that moved to London, and without fail, she won the hearts of more admirers.

In 1897, one such devotee sent a letter to the manager of Mabel's London show.

> Bachelor's Club. Dear Sirs I would like to offer my services in the part
> of Policemen in the "Belle of New York" as I now understand the part to be vacant.
> I shall be pleased to take this part without compensation.
> And you will do me a great personal favor by assigning it to me.
> Which I shall be happy to repay by any means in my power.
> I am 6ft high and think my experience as an army officer fits me to a certain extent for this part.
>
> Yours faithfully,
> Crichton

This young man was Lord Henry Crichton, an officer in the Royal Horse Guards, eldest son and heir of the Earl of Erne, the true *beau sabreur* of his generation. This was an era when our young British aristocrats were infatuated with the irresistible young American actresses appearing onstage, so who could blame the lovelorn lieutenant? "LOVESICK NOBILITY," alleged one headline I perused, but there really was a contagion of chorus girl syndrome in England at this time.

Henry demonstrated youthful tenacity, but to no avail. Maybe the army authorities objected to one of their most promising adjutants playing a policeman in a burlesque house in the evening. Lord Henry, not so easily thwarted, next chased, unsuccessfully, American Miss May Goelet, the twenty-million-dollar heiress. She audaciously suggested, in 1902, right before he shipped out for the war in the Transvaal, South Africa, that he should win a Victoria Cross before she would consider him worthy of her affections. Obviously, she was not impressed with his being merely the equerry for the Prince of Wales. Chivalry was alive in England. Viscount Crichton did go to war and returned, but only with a DSO and Queen's Medal and five clasps, thereby not fulfilling his quest. Instead, in 1903, he chose to marry Mary Cavendish, resulting, in rapid succession, the birth of a son and a daughter.

Reading the circumstances surrounding his death, I contemplated what a calamitous and fateful request Miss Goelet had made and often wondered if she ever gave a passing thought to the demise of her former suitor, that maybe he could have died trying to yet earn the Victoria Cross. In a freakish anecdote, not until 1916 was Crichton pronounced officially dead. It had been reported in 1914 that he was a German prisoner. In an unforeseen coincidence. Crichton married Mary Cavendish, sister of Lord Hugh Grosvenor, while Hugh married Crichton's sister, Lady Mabel Crichton. The pair of men would go to war together, be declared POWs, and both died at Ypres, Flanders, in Belgium together, just two of the fifty-eight thousand British casualties.

In a strange blend of comedy and drama, the former chorus girl arrived at a fortune. Miss Power's father was, at one time, a successful marble importer, prominent Boston businessman, and social figure. Mabel's uncle, Pierce Power, a prosperous Californian 49er gold miner without heirs, died in 1901 and left his estate of three million to his two Boston nephews, one of which was her father. Purportedly to be out of money and his fortune on ebb, her father, Richard, was found dead on the floor of the lodging house where he was residing. Providentially, Mabel inherited her father's half of the fortune. At the time of her father's death, she was singing her Salvation Army songs on a London stage. Naturally you already know how Mabel, Charley, Walter, the duke, and the earl ended. And think how innocent the golden girl's signature looked in our book. An Oom Cum Pivvy Sinkit to our Boston belle!

Outbound: Liverpool to New York, Day VI

Be just and fair to Everywomen, everywhere
Her faults are many, Nobody to blame.
—Patricia Collinge as Youth, London, 1912

Christmas on the *Maury* is always extraordinary. Everyone is more cheerful, even the ship seems to slice through the waves more smoothly. On 13 December 1912, Sir Ernest Kent (Kitten) and I looked around the table at our charmed circle. Frederick (TOM) and Alice Pauline (FLUFFY) Broxholm were going to America on a personal matter (I temporarily invoke the Order of the Three Monkeys again). Sir Kitten this night became enamored with the nubile eighteen-year-old actress Patricia Collinge (AH-NOOSO), or was it Crème de Menthe? Our married Kitten was smitten. Her recent acting in the play *Everywomen* at the Herald Square Theater on Broadway earned her a tidy $150,000. The production ran for 189 performances. Naturally, she played the role of Youth.

Most actors struggle with limited success, while others find fortune smiling upon them. At ten years old, Patricia's mother later relented and found her in a single scene at a Christmas bazaar at Balls Bridge in Dublin. Actress Moira Creegan saw her and thought she perceived possible latent talent. Armed with a letter to one of London's most respected actresses, Violet Vanbrugh, she was given a role as a Chinese doll in the play *Little Black Sambo*. She sang a song, danced a little, and her mom carted her back to Dublin and school.

The family moved to New York four years later. After spending several weary months looking for a stage play, an acquaintance directed Patricia and her mother to actress Bijou Fernandes, who sent her along to Thomas Ryley, who cast her at the last minute in his play *The Queen of the Moulin Rouge*. Noticed by an agent in the Shubert Theater Office, she was signed to a three-year contract and veritably pigeonholed. Immediately after being rediscovered, months later, she was cast as an understudy in *The Girl and the Wizard*.

One week later, the lead actress, Flora Parker, fainted ten minutes before curtain on Thanksgiving Eve. Thrust into the role, Patricia gave a creditable performance. Miss Parker returned for the next night's show, but people took note. Miss Collinge took the show on tour for a year. Fame and fortune onstage and screen would follow our blossoming Ah-Nooso for forty years. She wrote a poem.

Now I am a Heathen
And glad of heart am I
To emulate the Great Big Chief
I'll try and try and try . . .
(She added this line) "The first pain I ever felt when I cut a tooth,
But it will be naught to that I fear, when I have lost my youth."

To which I added at the end of the page: "Brother Kitten was this day raised to the Associate Order of the Yellow Buffoone, his behavior not appropriate this eve."

I am temporarily revoking the Grand Order of the Three Monkeys. The intertwining of the lives of my fellow Heathens has happened on occasion, frequently on the stage. I will reveal the incident concerning paternity. It concerns Frederick and Alice Pauline Broxholm and Arthur L. Pearse. Mr. Pearse was president of Arthur L. Pearse Consulting Mining Engineers in London. Additionally, he was a wealthy inventor, yachtsman, and world traveler from London. His boat *Carina* won several prestigious races.

Probably by the classical procedure, Fluffy became pregnant by the Little Chief while in London in 1907, but since Arthur was married to Mrs. Pearse, complications ensued. After baby Ethel Marian was born, Alice Pauline's mother gave the child to Mrs. Pearse—a very courtly English tradition. Mrs. Pearse took the child and raised Ethel as her own. In 1910, Mrs. Pearse became ill and went to visit her sister, Mrs. Parks, in Colorado. Upon Mrs. Pearse's death, Mr. and Mrs. Frank Parks cared for the child on their ranch in Rio Blancho. Late in 1911, Little Chief initiated legal action to obtain custody of five-year-old Ethel Marian in Grand Junction, Colorado.

Not to be outflanked, Fluffy Broxholm showed up in Grand Junction with her barrister husband, Frederick, claiming to be the real mother, and began proceedings to get custody. Providentially in June 1914, the Colorado Supreme Court ruled that the child should remain in the home of Mr. and Mrs. Park. Unfortunately, Barrister Broxholm's later troubles became public knowledge in England in 1928. Having committed several improprieties with clients' money, 1,300 pounds in one case, he was, as we say in Britain, struck from the rolls. Shortly after losing his law license, he was sentenced to six months hard labor, at Her Majesty's Pleasure. His excuse was that he found himself short of cash through no fault of his own and made the fatal step of going to a moneylender.

Interestingly, on the 8 December crossing, I had no inkling that our newly initiated converts, Frederick and Alice Broxholm, would, five days later, on December 18, be in a Colorado courtroom, filing custody papers. In 1917, the sixty-year-old Mr. Pearse would be involved in an incident wherein he was sued for fifty thousand dollars by the youthful Lillian Agnes Hennessy. Little Chief had decided no more little chiefs. He was sued for breach of promise of marriage in March 1912. Why did she wait five years? Perhaps it was fellow Heathen civility, Lillian had taken the tribal oath.

To the unknowing Lillian, Arthur was married to Catherine Jepson since August 1916 and living at the Hotel Ritz-Carlton in Montreal. Arthur admitted in court documents that he had made the marriage proposal to Lillian but asserted that in 1915, she canceled and rescinded the proposal. He later claimed he was jilted. Lillian's attorney, Jacob Eilperin, proclaimed Miss Hennessy was a woman of position, had no desire for publicity, and would not reveal her identity. The outcome of that case remains hidden from my best efforts, but our Little Chief managed to be constantly staking new claims.

Ever heard of the Pearsite Co.? Probably not since it only existed for two years, hoping to be a dye-making venture during the war. Two major plants were constructed. Colonel Henry Bope was the founder, and our Mr. Pearse was the vice president, even though the company used his name. Apparently Mr. Pearse, along with Californian chemist Dr. Charles Gage, had invented a revolutionary way of processing coal tar into finished dyes, freeing America from dependence upon Germany for them. The company collapsed in bankruptcy in 1917. There was no mention of Mr. Pearse.

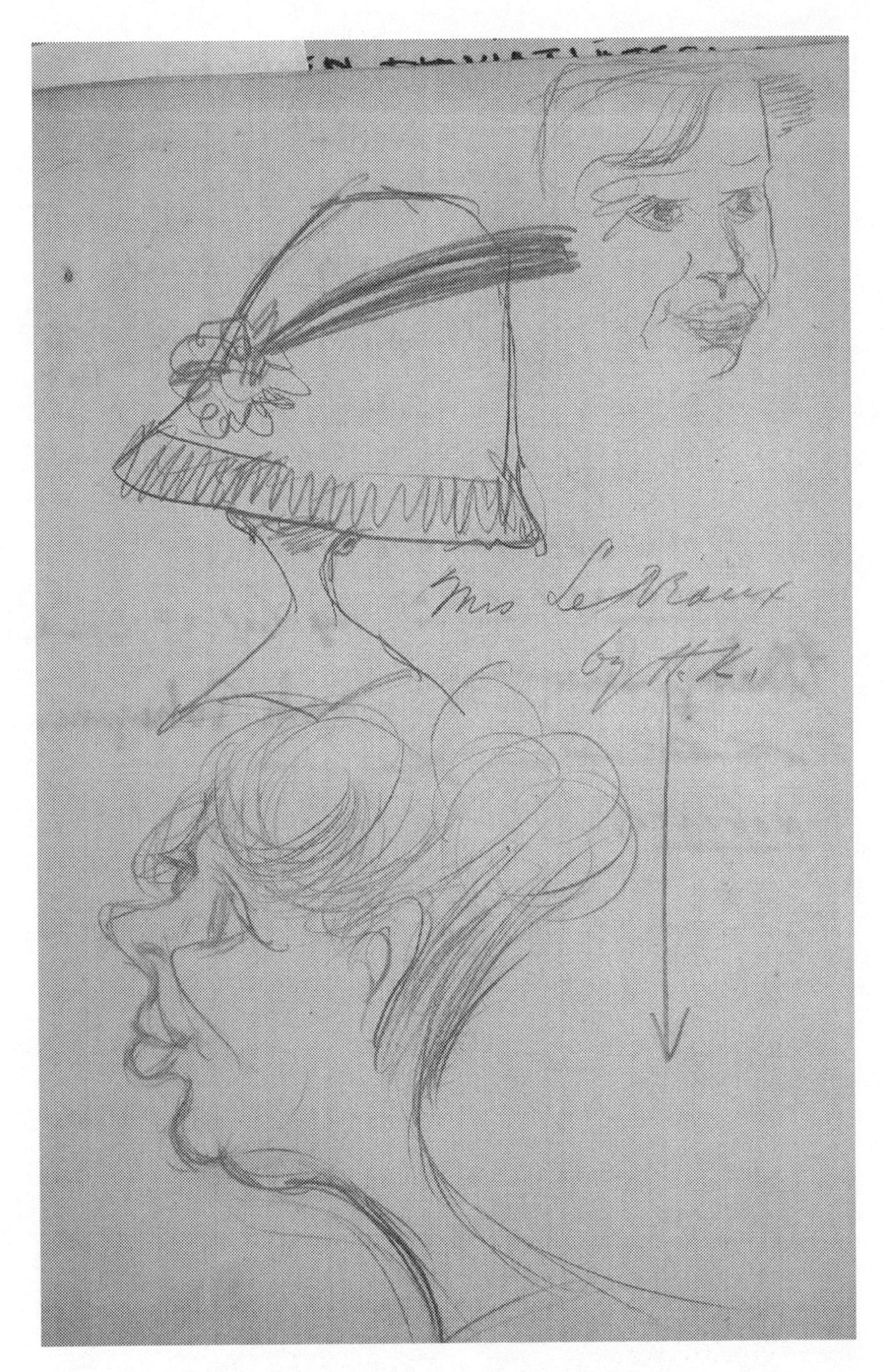

Ethelwyn Leveaux by Herbert Kaufman

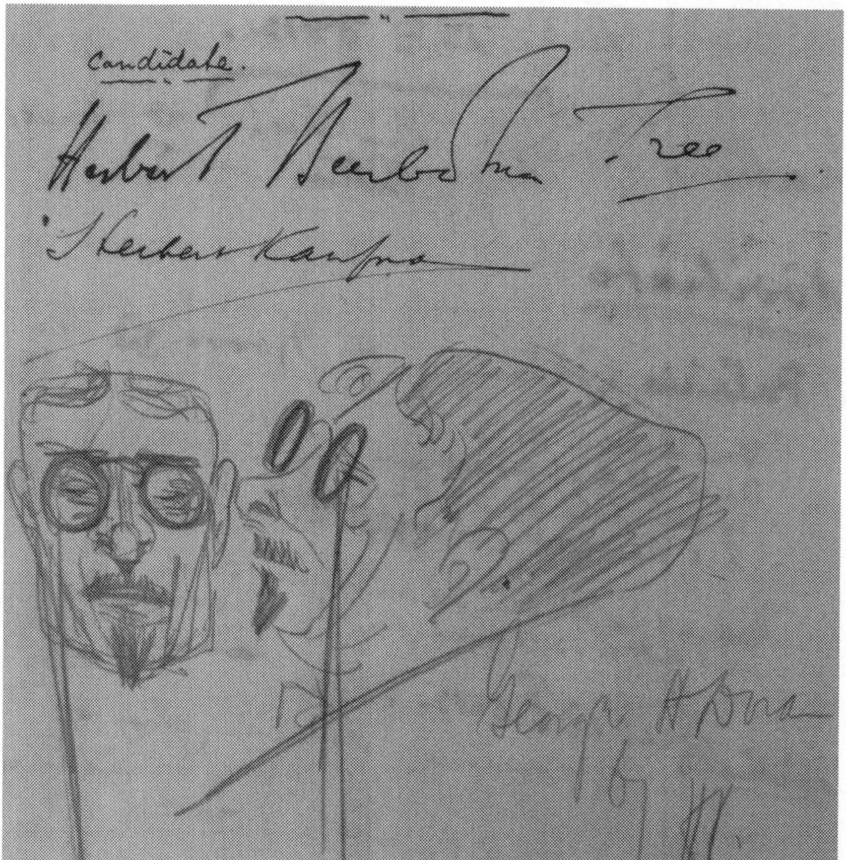

George H Doran by Hebert Kaufman

Frank Harris (top) & HK by Herbert Kaufman

Homeward: New York to Liverpool, Day IV

On December 21, I lost all control of the book. Actor Mr. Herbert Beerbohm Tree and novelist Mr. Herbert Kaufman were initiated. Mr. Kaufman became artist *extrordinaire.* He filled several pages with sketches of Mr. George Doran, Mr. Percy Morgan, a self-portrait, the enamoring Mrs. Leveaux, and me, Pills Jones. He called mine an idealization. I preferred to think of it as perfectly accurate.

The highest-paid writer of his era, second only to Teddy Roosevelt, Mr. Kaufman was a well-published novelist, editor, and newspaperman, with a large audience of devotees to his globally syndicated editorials. He stormed the country with the power of his pen, finding a strong appeal to men of all social classes. The popularly successful novel *The Winning Fight* of 1910 preceded his new book, *Do Something, Be Something,* which was just published and selling briskly. He had just recently accepted the post as editor and writer for the magazine *Woman's World.* Some mentioned the word *genius.*

> While Herbert's pen dashed off sanctimonious platitudes
> he couldn't make his own morals behave. It's too bad that men
> whose flesh is weak cannot refrain from preaching to other men.
>
> —*Oakland Tribune,* 3 May 1913

In unbridled irony to his fellow Heathens, he would divorce four months hence a fellow Heathen, his wife, Helen Kaufman. She accused him of having a relationship with another woman while she traveled in Europe last year. In court documents, Sister Kaufman stated that when she returned from Europe, she uncovered that her husband had been friendly with other women. Kaufman testified that he was lonesome and invited friends to call at his apartments.

The wedding was a surprise to the bride's close friends. In August, HK would marry the youthful society girl from Portland, Oregon, Alta Rush. Blessed with an exceptional voice, she had been studying music in New York for the past two years. Alta, additionally, was an accomplished equestrian. Does he know women or not? Well, at least half the time, readership may diminish at *Woman's World.* His career would not. He would be appointed assistant US secretary of the Interior in 1918. My favorite word of his was *dontgiveadamnedness*. He would write a poem titled the "Hell Gate of Soissons," about a 1918 battle in France during the world war. Ninety thousand men would die—not too terrible for the written word.

Sir Herbert Beerbohm Tree was one of the great luminaries of the British stage for decades and its undisputed leader since the death of the great Henry Irving. He acted onstage with many of his fellow Heathen heretics. Indeed a bona fide tribesman, he was simultaneously supporting an entire second family of six children in Putney, England, with the occasionally estranged May Pinney. Books about his successes have been written. Instead, I will give you one little story. He loved his wife, Helen Maud Holt, but was a notorious womanizer.

Our High Priestess, Constance Collier, had a cottage at Birchington-on-Sea, in Kent, England. In her book *Harlequinade*, she tells about the accident to Sir Tree. She had bought the cottage from fellow Heathen Lena Ashwell (Queenie). Herbert would appropriate the hideaway as needs dictated for work or his trysts. The old-fashioned cottage had a steep small winding staircase in the center and a handrail that ran the entire length of the stairs, but stopped suddenly with nothing to grasp. On a splendid summer day in 1917, Mr. Tree had the misfortune of falling down the stairs while at the cottage, fracturing his kneecap. He went to a London hospital, where, several days later, he died after having an operation on his knee. Most likely a heart attack was the culprit, as reports indicated he was of good disposition and recovering. Constance, who knew him well, stated that when Mr. Tree died, "a great deal of the magnificence of the British theater died too."

Homeward: New York to Liverpool, Day IV

The New Year began on 26 January 1913, as I recollect. The assembled devotees this evening were both daughters of the famous English playwright Henry Arthur Jones, Winifred (SISTER PEGGY) and Ethelwyn Sylvia (SISTER POKEYNOSE). Mr. Jones, always the devoted father, often cast them in productions of his plays. Joining our feast was Kurt Waldenstrom, a thirty-seven-year-old merchant, playing games of flirtation with the two glamorous women at our table. His brother Emil, traveling with him, was engaged in games of chance in the smoking room. Both ladies were married and traveling sans husbands, but it did not bother him in the least. The chefs concocted humorous names for our menu, as requested by our host, Mrs. Leslie Faber, listed here.

Grapfruit en Cave
Platipus a al PokeyNose
Orinthoincus a la Presse
Salad Stoneage
Bamboo Roots in Yellow Sauce
Petrodactyal Egg in Leau Feu
Fruit de Jungle
Pegge Potion

We were degenerating, and voraciously feasting on these strange concoctions.

Winifred was an accomplished actress on both the English and American stages and was married to noted actor Leslie Faber. She had just completed a substantial role in Charles Frohman's play *Bella Donna*. In 1915, I read that she was supposed to sail on the ill-fated voyage of our sister ship, the *Lusitania*, but canceled just before departure. Unfortunately, her friend, Charles Frohman, the famous theater producer, went down with the ship. One critic in *The Sketch* wrote that she "plays her parts with rare intelligence and distinction" and that he "hoped marriage does not end so promising a career."

Her sister, Ethelwyn, a voluptuous blond beauty, was, at the moment, married to Montague V. Leveaux, whom she wed on 22 April 1902, receiving no less than three hundred gifts! At that time, MV was two years out of Cambridge and the youngest of theater managers, presently at the Garrick in London. On the day of their nuptials, the *Yorkshire Post* wrote:

> In the history of the theater no young couple of its members
> have started life with more sincere good wishes for their true happiness.

Their marriage was, as we say in England, dissolved by a decree nisi in 1909. Our PokeyNose sued Monty on the grounds of desertion and misconduct, he was found living with a supplementary woman at the Hotel Surbiton in London. Monty was condemned by his handwriting in the hotel's register. In a strange contradiction, Ethelwyne begged him to reconsider his decision and recounted the unhappy passages of her married life, according to court records.

Where do I begin the tale of Ethelwyn? Let me start with the words of English author William Somerset Maugham from his 1930 novel *Cakes and Ale*, widely accepted to have been semibiographical: "When she liked anyone it was quite natural for her to go to bed with them. She gave herself as naturally as the sun gives heat or the flower her perfume . . . She was like a clear deep pool in a forest glade." He added, "She had grave and maddening faults . . . but she was beautiful and honest." Better words I could not compose myself, and, though I scarcely knew her, they coincided with my own thoughts. She was the only true female love of Maugham's life, and he had a seven-year affair with her, unusual for a man who, as he himself put it, was "three-fourths queer and one-fourth normal."

Finding myself a soothsayer in my unusual manner of existence, I can tell you that in the forthcoming November of this current year, Maugham would go to Chicago, where she was acting in a play. Previously, Maugham had gotten her a role in his play *Penelope*, later writing, "chiefly inspired by a young woman with whom I was having an affair." His sole purpose was to propose marriage on his visit, she refused. He returned himself and the ring to New York, costing him a 10 percent loss in the value of the ring and 100 percent loss in his once-hopeful heart.

Her brother Lucien Jones reported in his Chicago newspaper column that she was indeed secretly engaged to Maugham for a month, but subsequently broke it off, telling him she could not love him well enough to become his wife. Maugham always believed she was pregnant by a suitor as to the cause of his rejection (the skeleton in the closet in *Cakes and Ale* perhaps). In a letter to close friend and artist Gerald Kelly, Maugham wrote that in Chicago, Susan was found "in a very hysterical condition . . . [Maugham] can do nothing with her. Poor thing. Her nerves, her digestion, everything has gone wrong. It is an effect America has on people." Reading of her marriage twelve days later, Somerset guessed Angus McDonnell had made her pregnant: "I knew she was careless in these matters." Her brother Lucien later asserted the illness was caused by his sister's affection for Angus and angst at Maugham's proposal. The elated couple never did have any children.

In December of the same year, she secretly married the Honorable Angus McDonnell at the All Souls Church in Illinois, a wealthy and successful fruit rancher in Vancouver. Angus was the second son of the earl of Antrim and also involved in railroad construction. Having first seen Ethelwyn onstage in Doris Keane's play *Romance* from the front row in New York, he followed her to Chicago when the play traveled to that city. Angus proposed, and PokeyNose refused—several times. Repeatedly telling friends and family she would never marry again, he finally broke down her fading resistance. Sitting in the audience every night proved to be an expensive and successful courtship for the persistent earl. Nothing more affirming than a Heathen being ordained into the English peerage!

Maugham once wrote that "the memory of her lingered on in [his] mind, year after year" and that he never fully recovered from losing her to Angus. Maybe his memory haunted Ethelwyn. Her mark next to her name in the archive was similar to the one Maugham always placed on the front of his books, a Moorish symbol to ward off the evil eye. Just a coincidence, I am sure. Maugham cared for her so much that he commissioned the great English painter, Sir Gerald Kelly, to render her form on canvas, which was entitled *Mrs. Leveaux in White* in 1907. A head portrait Maugham ordered from Gerald always hung in his study, until his death. Not yet a sir, Gerald would become her lover and left for Burma when their affair came to an end in 1908 (an "odious treachery," Maugham wrote to his artist friend). The painting was breathtaking, just like the young lady herself. Unashamed, openly and innocently sexual, unstifled by respectability or class, she was a most irrepressible woman, born directly from the primordial elements themselves. In Ireland, in 1948, she returned to that ethereal place from whence she had come. She starred in her own real-life play, *Madame Sans Gene.*

In early February, a savage gale pounded our ship. Windows were smashed, railings twisted and detached in places. Dented metal plates on the forward hull were discovered. Lifeboats broke loose from their stanchions and had to be battened down by our stalwart crew. As the newspaper accounts reported, the one-hundred-miles-per-hour winds "gale tossed and wave pounded" the ship for hours. The most literate description I read was "Snarling and writhing in the teeth of the hurricane." There was a measure of humor as the few brave souls, having ventured out of their cabins in evening attire, were shocked when the waves smashed open the windows in the first-class lounge. To the captain's and surgeons' satisfaction, the ship and passengers arrived safely to port.

Homeward: New York to Liverpool, Day IV

On 9 March 1913, BIG CHIEF and SISTER ARIZONA welcomed Clarence Graff (GAMBIT) to the order. Clarence chose his mark, a knight chess piece, with forethought. He was wise enough to marry accomplished Canadian opera singer Florence Brimson, better known by her nom de theatre, Mlle. Toronta. One of Gambit's business ventures was managing Walter Damrosch, composer and conductor of the New York Symphony, who was featuring the rising young star. After marriage the handsome blonde with the fine voice retired from a promising career. She was a protégé of the great opera star Nellie Melba.

The elegant young soprano was the only child of a millionaire plane manufacturer. After his premature demise, the mother and daughter departed affluence to grapple with penury. Compelled to find work, she took a job singing in the Episcopal Church Choir. There she was discovered by wealthy New York patron, Mrs. Morrow, who financed her trip to Paris to study with the great opera coach Mlle. Marchesi. Voilà, a star was born. She was a rarity, described as "free of vanity and affectation so common in singers of prominence."

Gambit's father, G. E. Graff, had a stockbrokerage firm that went bankrupt in 1901. They were accused of misappropriating funds. Stocks were bought, and receipts were issued, but no shares were really purchased, $267,000 worth. The questionable accounts involved New York fire chief Nevins and ex–US senator McCarty. Settling for fifty cents on the dollar, they were back in business in 1902. What did the French novelist Honoré de Balzac say? "The secret of a great fortune made without apparent cause is soon forgotten if the crime is committed in a respectable way."

Our Clarence was a member in good standing on the NYSE and would soon be buying a seat on the Coca Exchange and, I'm sure, a fine chess player. He lived in London with his wife, Florence, who was active in a club for expats living abroad and banqueting friends. This year in November, American ambassador Page and his wife would be entertained at by the Graff's at their London residence. What is a knight without a queen?

Always an avid newspaper reader, the Dr Jones chanced to glimpse an article that concerned his dealings with famous German opera soprano Johanna Gadski. A judgment against him for $948.83 was rendered on account of a failed contract for a 1901 concert tour. Fingers in a lot of pies he had. In 1917, an item I espied was headlined "REGRETTED HIS MARRIAGE." After their marriage, Clarence told Florence he had made a mess of it and intended to make things as unpleasant as possible. Seventeen years later, Florence was weary of enduring his unprovoked behavior and filed for divorce in Oakland, California. Maybe the apple truly falls not far from the proverbial family tree. All must have eventually been forgiven because they reunited, left England again, and moved to Santa Barbara, California. While there, Florence and Clarence became founding members of the Music Academy of the West, and he its first president. Gambit played a different tune.

On this night, Sister Arizona (Ernestine Craig) was raised to Order of the Yellow Ribbon for her exemplary behavior in the absence of her new husband, Franklin Wheaton-Smith. She restores Heathen harmony after her father received the Order of the Yellow Buffoone.

A biting hurricane badgered us in late March. The first-class dining room was completely deserted, save for one brave young woman, Marguerite Skirvin, an Oklahoma City girl (hotels were named after her in her hometown). Her star was rising on the Broadway stage, currently in the play *What Ails You?* at the Criterion Theater. She played a gymnastic instructor and had to be in fine physical shape. My seasickness remedy really works better when you are fit. On the humorous side, the great explorer Sir Ernest Shackelton was on board, but he also canceled dinner this evening. An Oom Cum Pivvy Sinkit for Miss Skirvin.

> "Spirit hands, elusive as they are, at last have been caught in impressions made in plaster" Mrs. Mercy Cadwallader said after a recent visit to Europe. "When the medium goes into a trance a small trough of melted paraffin is prepared. The ectoplasm appears and through the medium the hand is

induced to enter the paraffin, leaving an impression which is afterward cast in plaster"

Pittsburgh Post

Outbound: Liverpool to New York, Day V

My future friends, the visitants of the afterworld, were hovering at the table the night of 5 June 1913. I shall introduce the orthodox people that materialized: Olive and George Vits, Albert J. Chandler (DEARIE), the Gartley family, WH, Helen, and Esther. Possibly normal was Antonio Deskens, but not yet determined. Unconventional, the final attendee, brimming with *personal e'lan,* was Mercy E. Cadwallader. I was mesmerized by the deep-blue eyes of the stunning American spiritualist. The preeminent celebrity reputedly possessed special gifts for communicating with forlorn phantoms.

George Vits began his business career as a tailor's apprentice for five years and a baggage handler for eighteen months. In a few years, he would be owner of Aluminum Goods Manufacturing Co. in Wisconsin, which, under his guidance, became the largest in the world. The company originally began as Manitowoc Aluminum Novelty Co., which was started by his father, Henry, and Uncle William (think utensils, cookware, and combs). The year 1911 was a pivotal year for the company's fortunes as they were awarded an eighty-thousand-dollar contract to make canteens for the army. Besides being an esteemed civic leader and progressive industrialist, he would be a national Republican committeeman and a wet delegate for repeal of the Eighteenth Amendment. That is why we liked him! George was an engaging conversationalist, as was his wife, and we were glad to have them on board.

Albert J. Chandler (Dearie) was a silk merchant. Antonio Deskens was a young man of mystery. A rumor that he was, in fact, the Marquis d'eskens de Frenoys, who had married a wealthy and much-older widow in Philadelphia named Mary Roberts circulated (she died in May 1915). Others intimated he had fled Europe in 1912 when rumblings of war began. His name made the papers in 1916 when the German government claimed he was a German citizen and accused him of leaving Paris when the German Army was mobilized, avoiding conscription. The

French confiscated his property. He claimed he was Belgian. He listed his nationality as Portuguese on his immigration form but had no appropriate accent. Undeniably, a mysterious personality.

William H. Gartley, an 1881 US Naval Academy graduate and president of the American Gas Institute, was from Philadelphia. He supervised many major gas installations across the United States when the industry was just in its infancy. We heard his wife, Helen, was one tough lady. In 1902, a burly burglar was located behind her bathroom door after the family had returned home from a social event. He threatened to kill her if she made a sound. As he attempted to escape, she grabbed him by the throat and called for help. In response, the burglar choked her nearly unconscious. The family arrived to find her on the floor, bloodied, bruised, and her clothing torn. The man jumped through a second-floor hall window, sixteen feet from the ground, to make his getaway. What a spunky lady.

The bewitching blueness of Mercy's eyes was the first thing you noticed. Peering into them, one could almost believe she really did talk to the deceased. Statuesque and entrancing, she projected a serene calmness about her person. A published author on the subject of spiritualism and editor/owner of the *Progressive Thinker* in Chicago, she was returning from England after holding a séance with Sir Arthur Conan Doyle. She would write several widely read novels on the subject: *Gems of Thought, Hydesville in History, Mary Vanderbilt, A Twentieth Century Seer*, among others.

Wandering the spirit world I came across a most unprecedented article from the Wilkes Barre Times. I shall use the author's own words, in places, from his interview with Mercy at Lily Dale, the Spiritualist Camp in Chautauqua County, NY in 1893. "This writer was astounded to discover a person graced with the lofty virtues of mind and character endowed with so much gentleness should have acknowledged her full and firm belief in the books statements." And she had "remarkable attractiveness with personal charm and mental ability." We agreed on the latter.

Antiquity Unveiled had just been published. In it, the author and publisher of the spiritualist journal *Mind and Matter* in Philadelphia, Jonathan. M. Roberts asserts, "Jesus of the Christians is a mythical character, chiefly based on the deeds of Apollonius of Tyna. Ancient voices from the spiritual realms prove Christianity is of Heathen origins. Mercy "disclaims any merit for the laborious and constant labor continued for over a year in carefully editing voluminous messages purporting to come from those who lived on earth prior to, during, and subsequently to the beginning of the Christian era". She must have been a zealous medium to sift through all the communications of those referenced in the book, especially since the author passed in 1888.

Prophetically, Big Chief knew begetting the Heathens had a tad of worthiness. Much of Christianity is adopted from pagan beliefs. Residing in the *Fortunate Isles* for the last 72 years, I can relay that man's diverse and contrived religions, although relevant to many on earth, are gravely misguided and little discussed. Hither, the conversations encompass the decency or indecency of humankind.

Mercy had a son Harry, of whom she was very proud. She wrote in the archive next to her name, a long sentence, but then obliterated the words with thick circles for reasons undetermined. (a prophesy, a secret enchantment, or curse?). Fascinated, I have tried to decipher it to the point of frustration, the legibility worse than my physician's gnarly scroll. In the one rare instance we get the leading, most well-known clairvoyant of our time to the table (I enticed her by promising genuinely primitive rituals), and not a séance was held. Perhaps it transpired and we were unaware. The other mortals present were not quite ready to fully embrace her talents. I missed a great opportunity.

Homeward: New York to Liverpool, Day IV

The guests are met, the feast is set, May'st hear the merry din.

—Coleridge

Irving Berlin and Cliff Hess left Tuesday on the *Mauretania*. Both sober.

—*Variety*, June 13

As all people traveling on the water know, you leave all your cares and worries on the dock. The sea emancipates your mind and casts all worry adrift. The night of 15 June 1913 was exemplary of that carefree emotion. It was an extraordinarily bibulous evening. The assembled brethren were Alice Lloyd (LITTLE MOTHER), Tom McNaughton (PHUNNY PHUNSTER), and their sixteen-year-old daughter, Alice

McNaughton (FLAPPER). Harriet Silverman (KARNOLS) and I rounded out the already anointed ones. Gathered to be initiated were Bessie Hyams (KIDDY), Harriet's young son, Sydne Silverman (SKIGIE), Milton Aborn (P), Franklin Wheaton-Smith (PICK AX), and John W. Kelley (VICTORIA). John was a machinist contractor on his way to Russia—I thought he was a spy! At long last, bringing some much-needed musical acumen were Mr. Ragtime himself, Irving Berlin (MUSICAL PIVVY), and piano man Clifford Hess (SOFT-PEDDLE PIVVY). I wondered if Irving's trick piano was in the ship's hold. My observation was that we had more talented theatrical trouper's sitting at our table than any other ship afloat that evening. Altogether, a very distinguished turnout for Alice's "seventeenth" birthday party.

Alice McNaughton would have an acting career in her mom's American shows and modest success in England. She became engaged in 1917 to Lieutenant Alden in the Flying Corps. Flapper would be hired to write a column for *Variety* under the nom de plume of ALICE MAC. Daughter Alice protested, "I've never written a line in my life," although well-educated at a private boarding school in England. The column ran for several years, entitled "Among the Women." She married John A. Keller at the family home, Sea Cliff, at Islip, Long Island, in 1953. She most thankfully did not have her appendicitis attack in my ship in 1916.

Broadway's revered lady with the flaming red tresses was our Harriet Silverman. She and her son were off on a three-week adventure to establish *Variety* magazine offices in Paris and London. Originally a Syracuse, New York, gal, her husband, Sime, brought her to the bright lights of his beloved street in New York, Broadway. Fired from the *New York Morning Telegraph* in 1905 for being too tough as a vaudeville reviewer, he borrowed $2,500 on the cuff from Hattie's father. *Variety* magazine was launched in 1905. While having late repast at Pabst's Casino in Harlem one night, she doodled the famous *V* that would adorn the cover of *Variety* on a napkin. She soon began to write a fashion column for the magazine under the name "The Skirt".

After many nights of experimenting with strong
glasses the following discovery was made by
~~the~~ musical Fairy. Prior to this no certain
reason was known for the young lady wearing a yellow ribbon round her neck — of course
she said something about a lover going
away — but we had our doubts.

Around her neck she wore a yellow ribbon
I tried to guess the reason till my brain was in a wreck
But soon I found beneath the yellow ribbon
She very very cleverly concealed a dirty neck.

(Rev. G. May)
Think it out.

Mysterious archive entry written by Irving Berlin

In 1907, Hattie persuaded Alice Lloyd, her closest friend from London, to sit down to lunch with Vesta Victoria, a popular fellow English actress. They had both come to America at the same time bringing similar shows, and the competition led to an estrangement. Hattie reunited the friends and led to an entente cordiale. When Alice had a box party for the opening of her husband's play in 1919, *The Magic Melody*, Hattie was there. Instinctively, Mrs. Sime was a surpassing hostess at home and for a hobby collected hats and vials of perfume. I can attest to the fact she had exquisite taste in both the latter. Columnist O. O. MacIntyre summed up her personality best:

> Loyal to the street her husband loved so well
> She encourages newcomers, steadies old timers,
> And has charted the course of many who have arrived,
> and as many more who are on the way up.

A true grande dame, she lived to be one hundred. She had a ruptured appendix in 1919 at her home, The Oregon, in NYC, not anywhere near Dr. Jones.

Skigie, at age seven, under that nom de plume, had written a column for *Variety* magazine that reviewed vaudeville shows. Today, at sixteen, he is a star athlete at St. John's Military Academy and an excellent student, telling me about his passion for fast cars and powerboats. Besides inheriting management of the magazine when his father died, he would become a noted powerboat racer in hydroplane boats named *Oh Boy* and *Yaka Hula*. Actress, budding film star, and dancer Marie Saxon took notice of this young man, so much so that she married him and gave up her promising career at its very height. The delicate Marie would die after a long illness at thirty-seven years old, and Sydney would die in 1942. They had a son, Sydney, who carried forward the banner of the family's heritage.

Withal I diverge farther from the party at hand, sundry revelations about Sime Silverman. New York mayor Jimmy Walker called Times Square as Sime's Square in reference to his broad reach. The man was everywhere that was anywhere. He lent money to anyone who asked, predictably picked up the checks at lunch or dinner, even giving away his car if someone liked it (of no help to me—I can't drive).

"A pass in perpetuity to Sime Silverman" was set in platinum and gold. The lifetime pass allowed attendance to more than half the shows in the world, over twenty-five thousand venues of amusement. Only one of those existed. He hated to travel.

Liquor, cards, cars—he spent three million fast. His most lasting legacy was the flinty words he left to the language. Words like *palooka, baloney, scram, pushover,* SA (sex appeal), *ah nuts, clicked, wowed* were seen first printed on the pages of *Variety.* The year 1915 was not a good year for Sime as he was sued by Charles Ahearn for alienation of affection of his wife, Vesta, in the amount of fifty thousand dollars. Baloney! In his will in 1933, he canceled all debts owed to him and left $2,500 to Sandra Lochs. Who was she?

> Egg Bill was the only witness of the killing of Hob Nob
> Reilly
> by Sheeny Ben Adleson in front of Nigger Mike's Place.
> —*New York Sun*, 1908

The amount of self-confidence surrounding the table was more than I had ever seen previously. We had the top star in music hall, Alice Lloyd, and the top songwriter, Mr. Berlin. He was on his way to England to sign a very nice contract for rag songs and appear at the London Hippodrome for a week, his first visit. Rather commendable for the former singing waiter at Nigger Mike Salter's saloon. Discovered by Henry Waterson there one evening, Waterson offered to finance him and put him in contact with music publisher Ted Snyder. Under the guidance of Max Winslow, Mr. Berlin was maneuvered from Bowery piano tinkling to Broadway spotlight. Musical Pivvy gave Tilly Winslow a twenty-thousand-dollar square-cut diamond in appreciation of her husband's efforts on Alexander's Ragtime Band (it sold three million copies in three months). Self-taught at the piano, he played almost exclusively in the key of F, which are the black keys. He once quipped, "The black keys are right there under your fingers. The key of C is for people who study music."

> "I suppose we all work best under pressure. I can't get to work until my partners tell me that sales are falling down, that the rent is increasing The salaries are going up-all because I am not on the job. I sweat blood. Absolutely I sweat blood between 3 & 6 many mornings. And when the drops that fall off my forehead hit paper, they're notes. I composed

> the melody and wrote the 1st verse of "International Rag" in the Hotel Savoy in London at 4 o'clock in the morning, the day before I opened. I threw all my bath towels into the piano to deaden It's resonance. I wrote the next verse the following morning and sang the song that afternoon. I wrote "Alexander's Ragtime" in 18 minutes surrounded on all sides by roaring piano's and roaring vaudeville actors."
>
> Irving Berlin
> *Theater Magazine*, Feb. 1915

Mr Milton Aborn was no second fiddle, being a top American operatic producer. He was returning from a European trip after contracting to produce the operas *Salome* and *Samson and Delilah* in English for the first time on an American stage. No one was surprised when he announced to the assembled PIVVY that he found the European music business honeycombed with graft and corruption. He was going to favor American singers over European whenever he could. When asked about his widely publicized contract dispute with actress Elsie Janis in 1907, much the gentleman, he merely said an amical settlement was reached out of court. Someone questioned (P) about his passing out while in the jury box during the trial of Alderman Henry Clay Peters. The ex-politician was on trial for perjury. Mr. Aborn replied it was not the extreme heat but Mr. Peter's terrible acting that forced him to be carried from the courtroom.

One could not pick up a newspaper in America from 1890 to 1933 and not see the Aborn name. He, and his brother Sargent, specialized in comedic and revivalist opera, like Gilbert and Sullivan, at reasonable prices and, most importantly, used excellent talent. At age twenty-one, Milton was pressed into service as an actor on a Boston stage for a performance in the *Tourists* when an actor became ill. Mr. Aborn suddenly found he had more talent as a manager. Later he decided to produce, but found himself in multiple roles; director, stage manager, rehearsal supervisor, and actor. He applied his indefatigable energy to ensure the success of his productions. Amidst his busy life, Milton found time to marry Marjorie and raise two daughters. Operagoers across the United States can thank him for bringing quality productions to their towns.

Utilizing my recently acquired gift of prophecy is such great fun. Franklin Wheaton-Smith (Pick Ax), a mining engineer from Minnesota, owned gold and silver mines, and was married to Anna Ernestine Craig, now Smith (Sister Arizona), who would bear him a son and daughter. Does the "law of apex" bring forth any latent memory? It will not, unless you were a miner in the 1870s. In the United States, the law allowed miners extra-lateral rights to follow a vein horizontally, undeterred by trespassing on another's claim. The vertical lines of the claim projected down into the earth did not cut off the vein as it did in other countries, as Mr. Smith's article in August 1916's *Mining Magazine* pointed out. In 1937, the fifty-seven-year-old Pick Ax was included in the who's who of mining, a prestigious albeit obscure, honor.

Bessie (Kiddy) was a graduate of the Metropolitan Opera School in New York. The rising young star sings in a sweetly melodious soprano voice or speaks in a monologue during unique operatic recitals while playing the piano. She almost sings when she talks. Miss Hyams was going to England, where her father was a horse trainer at Epsom Downs, outside of London and owned a racehorse named Maori Star. She would be acting in a amateur dramatic performances while in England, and, unknown to her, she would be attending her aunt Marie Lloyd's wedding to famous jockey Bernard Dillion the coming February. You correctly guessed that our Alice Lloyd was Marie's younger sister.

Nineteen-year-old Cliff Hess began as a railroad boy in Cincinnati and started playing piano on Mississippi riverboats at sixteen, near his hometown. He had recently been recruited by Mr. Berlin as a personal assistant, accompanist, private secretary, and manager. Irving could not read or write music, but he was masterful at tunes and lyrics. Soft Pedal Pivvy would have a long career as an executive at several recording and publishing companies, in addition to the many hit songs he would soon write. He did the short film, *Ready to Wear*. In 1927, he married Dorothy Holmes Morosco, theater owner Oliver Morosco's sister-in-law. Musicians, actors, comediennes, an opera producer, a mining engineer, and one ship's doctor, the mackerel was holy tonight.

The Heathens this night raised SISTER SILVERMAN to the Order of the Yellow Ribbon. Amid sobs of joy, Brother Berlin was elected MUSIVAL PIVVY, with orchestral accompaniment by the Pivvys present. "Blod guess us," the PHUNNY PHUNSTER.

"There's many a slip twixt the cup and lip"
Theodore Roosevelt (his diary 1879)

The strangest entry in the archive was written this evening, and I know not when. I will leave it for you to decipher its cryptic message.

After many a nights experimenting with strong glasses
The MUSICAL PIVVY made the following discovery
Prior to this no certain reason was known for the young
Lady wearing a yellow ribbon around her neck, of course
She said something about a young lover going away,
But we had our doubts.

Around her neck she wore a yellow ribbon and I tried
To think of a reason till my brain was in a wreck
But soon I found that beneath the yellow ribbon
She very very cleverly concealed a dirty neck.
—Ren G. May
(think it out)

As you can imagine, I did not immediately know the author, nor to whom it was ascribed, and affirming the culprit took a wee bit of sleuthing. Discovering sheet music of a new Irving Berlin song from 1913, entitled "Pullman Porter Parade," the cover asserted the author as Ren G. May. Musical Pivvy had a dispute with his publisher and wrote several songs using that name (anagram for Germany). So Mr. Berlin wrote the two paragraphs, but about whom? We had one yellow ribbon given out on this voyage, to the wife of Irving's poker-playing pal Sime Silverman, Mrs. Harriet Silverman. Did dining, drinking, and dancing become more than flirtation? Was her mark (a carrot) and nickname KARNOLS symbolic of something ominous? Or was her meaning just about a vegetable? He took the time to write those lines. He put pen to paper, hence, without a doubt, it should have meaning. Sime had a unique lifestyle. He did once say, "Married life, not a war play." The sacred tome was signed by all and put to sleep, weary from a long but musical night. Big Chief fears he is beginning to lose his ballast.

HEATHEN NOVIATIATESION
JUNE 15th 1913

HEATHENS PRESENT

Alice Lloyd.
(LITTLE MOTHER) Peasant

Sydney Jones Big chief his mark.
Karnols Harriet F. Silverman Tom McNaughton P.P.
His serol
Alice McNaughton
Flapper

NOVIATIATES ?

Irving Berlin (musical Pivvy) 619.
Bessie Hyams (Kiddy) 620
Sylvia Silverman (Skigie) 621
William Morris (P) 622.
Franklin Wheaton Smith 623.
J. Kelly Victoria 624.
Clifford Hess (Soft Pedal Pivvy) Secy 20 625

Sister Silverman was raised to the order of the yellow ribbon [illegible] of Ivy. Bro Berlin was elected musical Pivvy with orchestral accompaniment by the Heathens present. [illegible] guess we
Phunny Phunatic
Tom Mc

Homeport: Liverpool: Respite October 1913

King George and Queen Mary were aboard, literally, for a royal visit. We did have a royal suite, but alas, they were only here for a short inspection of the *Maury*. I know in the colonies Americans cannot understand we Brits' adoration for the royals, so I will not expound further. The crew reveled in the prestige accorded our ship as being in the post of honor. The ceremony was for the dedication of the Gladstone Dock in Liverpool and the merchant shipping review. I later read the number of ships, mercantile and military, numbered more than twice that of the Spanish Armada of 1588—we had much better weather than the Spanish fleet received.

In August, the *Mauretania* had her first serious challenge for the Blue Riband. The new French liner, the SS *France*, had hoped to dethrone the *Maury*. The race began with the ships just three hundred yards apart in Liverpool harbor. Nearly the entire crossing toward New York the ships were in sight of each other, at times within shouting distance. I am happy to report our ship beat the SS *France* to Ambrose Light, which marks the entrance to New York and New Jersey harbors. Not by much, though, twelve minutes separated the two boats after four days on the ocean. A hardy hip hip hooray for the crew!

August was the month for a big shipboard event. Several crew members were spreading rumors about a big baccarat game going on in the smoking lounge. The third time it reached my ears, numbers like hundred thousand were being bandied about. I sauntered toward that room myself to separate smoke from mirrors. The game was still going on, and a crowd was gathered around one table. There was a lot of money on that table, in loose piles temporarily resting in front of two of the players. One player won two hands in a row for five thousand dollars each. I chose to linger table side no more, time to patent my seasickness remedy.

Homeward: New York to Liverpool, Day II

On September 11, BROTHER SANDOW and BIG CHIEF welcomed Canadian tourist Maud Denison (SISTER BUNNY), Leon J.

Garcey (BROTHER FULL MOON), and Baron Aleck Hochwaechter (BROTHER IGGY). You can guess by now who was the better looking of the group, by far Sister Bunny. She and her sister Dorothy were constant Canadian Tourists. The baron was living in New York and working on Wall Street, when not acting as escort for the reigning German prince when he visited. Brother Iggy did manage to get arrested for an automobile speeding ticket in NY in 1909. In October, two years later while crossing with us, the charming Baron was escorting Beatrice Graham White. The sister of the famous aviator, and our former fellow traveler Claude, was rumored at the time to be flying into marriage with our Brother Iggy.

Leon J. Garcey was his American name. Square-jawed with brown hair and a ruddy complexion, he looked Belgian. In France, he sported the name Count Joseph Reygon deau de Gratresse. Brother Full Moon had been admitted to our order in 1910. Referring to himself as a French civil engineer, he dabbled in railroads. Certain stories made the newspapers.

In 1905, he and his wife, a woman described by others as a surpassing beauty, were trapped on the top floor of the Metropolitan Tower, a New York City building he owned. His business was on the lower floors, his residence on the top. They were seen looking out of the window as the fire raged below them. Witnesses saw flames catch Mrs. Garcey's nightgown on fire, and Leon ran to her aid and began to beat out the burning clothing. Simultaneously, a fireman entered the upper window by ladder and wrapped his rubber fire suit around Leon's wife. Fireman Gregor picked her up and carried her down the ladder; Leon followed. She was lucky as most of the damage was to her hands, but not overly severe. The discerning doctor concurred that she was a striking woman.

The count was a US representative from France for French and Belgian railroad interests in the New World. In 1907, he arranged for then–secretary of state Taft's journey by rail to Saint Petersburg, Russia. He was a member in good standing at the Engineers Club, had a well-documented résumé on his expertise in the railroad business, yet often patronized numerous Broadway taverns.

Brother Full Moon was homeward-bound, his wife having just filed for divorce days earlier. In January, four months from now, his life would be laid bare in an American courtroom. Much to the discerning mind of the physician, it was confusing. Our count was caught by an agent of the apartment building in the room of different woman. He introduced this lady to the agent as the countess, who was clothed merely in dressing gown and slippers. In truth, Madam LeComte was technically a countess, but not *the right* countess, at least not yet. *Variety* magazine called her a "regular prima donna, a statuesque blond, cultured, pleasant to listen to, who dances gracefully" right into a married Heathen's arms.

The divorce suit reported that the first countess's jewelry was missing, except the ring on her finger. The other woman had been lavished with railroad passes, jewelry (whose?), and Pullman berths. He was paying for the other woman's divorce suit as well. In the midst of this entanglement, the count showed up at the real countess's room at 4:00 a.m. and demanded that she sign a divorce paper, withdrawing any claim to his fortune. Under duress, she signed, and he proceeded to evict her from her apartment, giving her twenty-five dollars to pay for a room elsewhere. Brother Full Moon was indeed a big spender. The court, recognizing the poor conditions to which the Countess Marie had been subjected and the humiliation of her forced eviction, threw out the original document. The judges awarded her the seventy-five thousand dollars in her suit, plus fifty-dollar-per-week alimony. She was allowed to keep the one jewel "no longer so" Full Moon had given her while courting in Switzerland many years ago.

He reconciled with the first countess, Marie. To my amazement, they would travel extensively and remain together. I spied them on the *Aquitania* once but failed to get the traditional Heathen greeting—I imagine I was invisible or he was not seasick.

As a rule, it is not well mannered to discuss smuggling. It is common knowledge that many passengers attempt to dupe the tax man, they simply do not want to pay the exorbitant duties on imported goods purchased abroad, most often women's clothing. On this trip, arriving in New York on 4 September 1913, twenty trunks were seized and inspected, and nearly five thousand dollars of imported and undeclared goods were found. The duty due was three thousand dollars. (I said exorbitant) The humor in this event was that the owners of the luggage were one Mrs. Frank Wiborg and her daughters, she being the wife of the assistant secretary of commerce and labor Frank Wiborg during the Taft administration. Mrs. Wiborg had to appear in court and claimed the items were purchased by her daughters without her knowledge (*Where did the money come from?* I wondered) and that there was no deliberate attempt to defraud Uncle Sam. She paid $1,750 in fines.

Forgetfulness can be expensive. We Brits love a good laugh, especially about a belabored labor secretary on Labor Day.

Dr. Sydney Jones chooses to narrate this account with mild trepidation as the principal player, the beloved sister of our favorite founder, and is not a member of the sacred order. If not told now, it may well never be, so I shall proceed. Time has been generous so far, and I will take advantage of the liberty to venture further into our provisional imperishability.

Alice Lloyd, had ventured back to America in the middle of September, and there was no offering to the gods of the sea. Alice would need her energies for an extended Western US tour and three months in Australia. She would expend loving aid when her sister Marie Lloyd, the "Queen of Comedy" in England, returned to America for an engagement at the Palace Theater, New York, opening on October 13. Marie had arrived on the *Olympic* on October 1, and Alice had gone down to meet her. As they were preparing to depart, an immigration inspector asked Marie if the traveling companion she had shared a cabin with on the promenade deck was her lawful husband, as they had been traveling as Mr. and Mrs. Bernard Dillion. Marie replied, "No, he is not my legal husband."

Her legal second husband was British entertainer Alex Hurley, and although Marie had filed for divorce, the courts in Britain had thus far refused to grant the decree. Victorian mores, laws, and public opinion being what they were, it was a serious offense. The inspector told her to get back on the *Olympic* and wait until the next morning to go to Ellis Island for an appearance before a Special Board of Inquiry. Then, realizing her predicament, Marie became hysterical and began weeping. Alice reached into her valise and out popped a bottle of champagne, the Heathens' prized beverage, after which Marie had savored, recovered, and walked back up the gangplank.

Byron Uhl, acting commissioner of immigration, said the actress was being charged with living with a man who was not her husband. Bernard Dillion, a twenty-four-year-old jockey who was one of Britain's best riders until recently suspended, was charged with bringing a woman here for immoral purposes (I thought most of the immorality had already transpired). Supposedly, the forty-three-year-old Marie was going to be paid $1,500 per week for forty weeks, including a stint at the Orpheum on the Pacific Coast, and that she was still married to second husband, vaudevillian actor Alex Hurley. "Barred from America" and labeled undesirable, the headlines read. *Good publicity*, I thought. In those more civilized days, society had strict code. Moral turpitude and depraved behavior shocked the conscience of civilized society, at least publicly.

Marie and Bernard were taken to Ellis Island and spent thirty-six hours under guard. Exhibiting solid sisterly devotion, Alice was able to secure their release by posting bonds of $1,500 for her sister and added $1,500 for Mr. Dillion. An appeal for special dispensation was sent to acting US Labor Secretary Post. After some deliberation, Secretary Post, probably in response to Marie's quote in a paper saying "They should remove the Statue of Liberty from its pedestal," sent a telegram to Ellis Island ordering a temporary landing until March 1914. It allowed Marie to fulfill her contracts, providing they lived apart. *Now just who was going to enforce that clause* the ship's doctor contemplated? Captain Herbert Haddock of the *Olympic* did comment to a newspaper how steadfastly and tirelessly Alice had worked to secure Marie's release. That's why Alice Lloyd was always held in my highest regard.

Not being a Heathen by initiation herself, Marie Lloyd's eight months of adventures on the continent were just beginning, and Big Chief deems them worthy of recounting. Her act opened at the Palace in New York to great fanfare, as would be expected. On the October 24, 138 crew members from the *Olympic* went to see Marie at a show and supported her with constant rousing cheers throughout the performance. In London, the search was on for the culprit who had cabled the American authorities as to Marie's matrimonial troubles. Never determined by the Lloyd clan, most likely, it was a reporter looking for a story.

Not to be surpassed, in November, Marie's daughter, actress Marie Courtney, obtained a divorce from her husband, Harry Aylin, another horse jockey. On November 25, Marie, the elder, sprained an ankle on the way to the theater and canceled her show, one of many excuses she would use for the next several days as she missed more shows. By December 7, Edwin Albee of United Booking Agents, had enough and summoned Marie to his offices. Timing in acting being what it is, Marie rode the elevator with Mr. Albee, not hearing his name, and complained vociferously how she didn't like her billing on the program. Reaching his offices, he terminated her contracts citing the slipshod manner in which she sang her songs and her chronic absences. Without contracts, she could be deported.

Martin Beck of the Orpheum Circuit again came to the rescue of a Lloyd sister. On December 6, Marie was informed that husband Alex Hurley had died of pneumonia in England. By December 11, Marie was performing in Chicago, where on the twentieth, she would marry Bernard Dillion (that didn't happen), now referred to as her manager. By January, Marie was performing in Canada. In Winnipeg on January 15, Miss Lloyd accidently seared her face with carbolic acid while removing grease paint after a show. The young messenger boy she had sent to the local druggist had forgotten what she requested, and then asked a rival actress what to get, rather than return to Marie empty-handed. The prescription written down by the other actress was for the carbolic acid. Fortunately, no serious harm was done.

On February 7, after being outraged by her review in the Vancouver papers, she strutted into the editor's office of the offending paper, Louis B. Taylor. Removing a concealed horsewhip from her muff, Marie proceeded to strike him three times with the leather strap and buckle. The paper had written that the act was clever but suggestive in gestures and actions. (To my knowledge, that *was* music hall.)

As you get on in years you cannot continue to wear baby clothes &
try and be funny. You must advance with age. Don't go onstage
and try and fool the public.

—Marie Lloyd to Alice Lloyd

Border guards being what they were, Marie and Bernard were again refused entry into America. Marie sent a telegram to immigration commissioner Caminetti, who responded, "A four-thousand-dollar-bond for Marie to enter the United States and $1,522 for Mr. Dillion," who was being held in detention because of paperwork in Vancouver. Marie went on ahead to perform in Portland on the sixteenth but was hissed off the stage and went into hysterics. In the interim, a further stipulation was demanded from Mr. Dillion: marriage or deportation. Marie said, "It is unlucky to marry anyone you love, but it is one way of meeting conventions." Under supervision of the British consul Douglas Erskine in Portland, Oregon, Marie and Bernard were married a second time by a Catholic priest at the British Consulate. February 25 found her headlining in San Francisco, and on March 15, she was in Oakland.

Perhaps lack of marriage ailed sweet Marie because she continued to entertain successfully until June. Marie and Bernard returned home. Marie would suffer a seizure and die a few years later in 1923 while performing onstage while singing the tune "Oliver Cromwell."

Big Chief Surgeon Jones will elucidate those who have followed this far on Phunny Phunster and Little Mother, who always will hold a special place in the old doctor's heart.

Alice Lloyd's Personality

There is no substitute for her.
Either you see Alice Lloyd or you do not. Miss Lloyd has
in addition to a marked cleverness, a distinct personality.
In other words she is herself and that makes her. To listen
to her character ditties, topical numbers, ballads or
whatever
it is she may be singing, is, in point of fact, to be regarded
in the light of
a special favor. There is a vein of broad humor comingling
with
a certain sauciness of demeanor, a chic movement and a
lively
step, and these things make the sum total of her
personality.

When Alice returned to a stage she had visited before it
was like
the meeting of more than an acquaintance. It had the
flavor of
a welcome.

—*Manitoba Free Press*, 21 February 1921

She has what the analysts call "magnetism,"
Nobody knows what this is, but she has it.

—*San Francisco Chronicle*, 23 April 1912

Better words than the Big Chief could prescribe. All of Alice's great North American achievements almost never happened. When, in 1907, New York theater owner Percy Williams first contracted for a female English music hall singer, he was under the impression that he had secured her more noted older sister, Marie. The communication from his man in London read; "Can send Lloyd by next steamer. Am confident she will make big success." Percy replied, "Send Lloyd to open at Colonial immediately upon arrival." Advertising matter was prepared. Alice sent a cable announcing her departure from Liverpool, and it was signed Alice Lloyd. Realizing his error, he immediately engaged another headline act from London, and Alice was temporarily forgotten.

No one met her at the pier. Monday morning came, and Alice went to the theater quietly and diffidently rehearsed her songs with the orchestra. She came onstage for her matinee performance, and by the third song, she had the audience completely at her feet. Encore followed encore until seven songs had been sung. Alice's star was born. It twinkled brightly for over twenty-five years on the continent.

> 12 years ago Alice Lloyd so electrified Broadway vaudeville on Monday Afternoon that her name was in electrics outside the Colonial Theater that same night. That made her a headliner in a day. She has been a headliner ever since.
>
> Sime Silverman, *Variety*, 14 November, 1919

Near the end of her career touring Alice was making $7,500 per week, a long way from the twelve English pounds she made for a week dancing with her sisters, Marie and Rosie, as the Sisters Lloyd at Barnard's Palace in Chatham in 1880. The girls chose the name Lloyd from the London bank, their last name being Wood. There she became friends with a youngster named Charlie Chaplin and where her sister Rosie's husband, Billy Pulaski, gave Charlie his first instruction in stage work. She packed theaters in the United States, Canada, Australia, New Zealand, and South Africa, a true tour de force, but never found the same success in England. Maybe it was due to older sister Marie's popularity with English audiences. Alice was always in her shadow on our island.

A large dinner party was gathered at Rector's Restaurant,
NYC, April 1907
In attendance were Tom & Alice McNaughton, brother
Fred McNaughton,
Mr and Mrs Sime Silverman, the Will Evan's, the Jack
Lorimar's, D.J. Casey, et al.

Anna Held and husband Flo Ziegfeld were seated at
another table.
Anna and Alice exchanged greetings. Flo offered Alice
$2500./wk
to play under his management. Former engagements
prevented
consideration of the tender.
—Sime Silverman, *Variety*, 13 April 1907

In 1910, Alice's American fame made her an obvious choice for the new Kinemacolor films (they were expensive and projectors were costly). She made one at home, in her gardens on Long Island, and the other, on the *Mauretania*, her favored ship, I surmised. Alice had the honor of being the only vaudeville star to adorn the cover of the prestigious *Theater Magazine* in 1912 for her heartily cheered role in *Little Miss Fix-It*. FLAPPER, her daughter, acted in the very same play with her mom. Seldom-mentioned is fact that our Little Mother adopted stage star Lily Lena when Lily's mother died. She continued her theater education. Early in Lena's career, she was billed as "serio" and dancer, the former being an abbreviation for seriocomic, where the artist presented a mixture of serious and comic. Miss Lily had great success.

Miss Lena's real name was Alice Mary Mathilde Archer, born in 1877. First married to William Newhouse she danced forward to Stanley Archer "Dick" Turpin, whom she divorced in 1919, the grounds, cruelty. Her career shined and then faded rapidly, near the end being labeled the "fashion plate comedienne" by the Washington Post.

Dr. Jones, being a man of medicine rather that the other way around, the only reason being a formal education, always took a keen interest in the strange machinations of the law profession. In 1918 Lily Lena sued the owners of the Victoria Palace Theater in London, the grounds, "loss of publicity". During rehearsal for her opening in March, 1917, she was unhappy with her allotted place on the program. Arguments ensued, Lily ascertaining that the program change would be "injurious" to her position as a "star" artist. Lily left the stage, going to her doctor to get a statement certifying that she was unable to perform because of a medical condition. Sir George Askew, producer, introduced a contract for vaudeville actors in 1911 that became the industry standard, specifically in this case. In Clause 11, the word "engagement", by custom, is referring to the particular week, not the entirety of booked dates, in this instance from 1917 to 1920. Without further demands of the reader I will reveal that the jury awarded Lily 100 ponds for salary and 100 pounds for publicity. What fine laws we have in England. I do wander around the compass for the full 360 degrees in our tale do I not?

Where were we.. It is said all actors are superstitious, and Miss Lloyd was no exception. On opening night, she always wore a white lace dress given to her by her grandmother. On her dressing table was a little black porcelain pig without front legs, which had been broken off when an Irish woman tossed it to her on the gangplank when she first sailed to America, saying "Good luck to ye always, darling." That charm worked beyond anyone's imagination.

Two small flags were placed on either side of her dressing mirror: on one side, a Union Jack; the other, the Stars and Stripes. In the center hung a little golliwog given to her by a little girl long before she left England. Her preferred piece was a diamond brooch given to her by New York society matron Mrs. Stuyvesant. Adorning her little finger was her infallible talisman, a golden ring given to her by a South African potentate. The ring was crafted precisely in the shape of a wishbone, and the only piece of jewelry Alice never removed.

Alice was wealthy but lost much of it in the US stock market crash in 1929. Her extravagance was the latest fashion in Paris, one dress for each song. She and Tom had second daughter, Grace *Tomme* McNaughton, born in July 1916 in America. They had homes on Long Island and in Barnstead, England. On the Thames, they had a houseboat named *Tomme*. Their home in England was named Little Trees, after Tom's famous recording of "The Three Trees." Always looking after others, Little Mother did bond sales and war shows in both her favorite homes, England and America. Alice and Tom traveled with me on the *Aquitania* several times, and on one voyage in 1922, she possessed fifty-eight trunks, which aroused no suspicions from the dry agents (liquor prohibition police). Alice loved to giggle and loved to laugh. A physician has nothing comparable in his bag.

"Customary mood of levity, full of quips and the little
verbal twists
and surprises that put him among the most legitimately
laughable

of the musical comedy buffoons." About Tom and Fred McNaughton.
—Percy Hammond, *Chicago Tribune*, 10 February 1914

Phunny Phunster chose his name well. Starting as the Two Macs with his brother Fred in the English provinces in the 1880s, they were soon celebrated throughout their native land as capable comedians with a genuine sense of humor and brilliant repartee. Both Tom's and Alice's parents and grandparents were on the stage. Tom was onstage at the Drury in London at four years old. Alice's London debut was in *Babes in the Wood* when she was fourteen. Tom met Alice because they were often booked on the same programs in the early years. To quote Tom,

> I played the front legs of a donkey for more than a year in one
> English play. I have never cared much for donkey's since, but that
> particular one could be hungry and express emotion and sorrow.
> The fact that Miss Lloyd afterward married the front legs of that donkey
> would seem to indicate that there must have been possibility in him.

Phunster soon got bookings in America with his brother (they would go their separate ways in 1910 after twenty-three years together) along with Alice, but his recognition never achieved that of his beloved Alice—few entertainers of the time did. He played to his biggest crowd ever, nearly six thousand folks by some estimates, in a famously hilarious charity Pantomime Football game in Huddersfield, England, in 1892 (whenever possible, he performed for charity). Tom was one of the most respected comedians of his day, being elected King Rat of the Grand Order of Water Rats in 1904, a London-based actors group based on fraternity and philanthropy. Tom was honored by his peers, being a member in both the Lambs Club and the Eccentrics.

> Tom had a clever trick to entice patrons into the theaters. He would place

a large advertisement in the local papers offering $1000 to
the local
Mayor if the Keith Theater manager could provide a
contract that paid
$2000 for his appearance.
—Cleveland *Plain Dealer*, 1909

Tom would produce Alice's programs, and despite his getting great parts in major shows himself, he declared bankruptcy in December 1913. The amount of $157,000 was quite an accumulation of debt in our time. I later discovered that Tom was a silent partner with Mark Leuscher and Weber in their agency, which had fallen into bankruptcy. The Werba/Luescher shows were extremely large and costly, often employing hundreds of actors. I found it funny (or sad) that on topping the debtor's list, Miss Alice Lloyd was owed thirteen thousand dollars, and, at the bottom, Mr. Hepner, the wig man, ninety-four dollars. Obviously, Tom was too busy acting to bother with accounting. It must have been a rough few weeks at home for the King Rat.

Introducing the *X-ray Dance*, Tom and William Morris created this unique production for Alice's US Dance Mad tour in 1914. It required six men operating intricate electrical equipment. It went like this:

The dancers are clad in white silk and diaphanous veiling's
Floods of light are aimed from every possible angle
The rays of light are so focused that where the rays meet
The effect is as near the actual scientific x-ray as the
theatrical
Producer could or would dare to show for purposes of
entertainment.
No one has ever criticized the dance as improper
But it has been reviewed as the most daring of the era. The
coloring
And lighting effects change during the progress of the
numbers
To produce various effects by the penetrating lights of
different
Colors and powers. To enhance the spectacle the dancers
Costumes are wired with insulated current carriers from
Batteries so small that the women concealed them in

their hair and the man his pocket. The dancers are
especially imported from England for the American
revealment
which has been copyrighted by William Morris.
—*Wayne Sentinel*, 24 January 1914

After matinee shows, Alice personally led dance classes on the Dance Mad tour. No other star did that for their audiences.

Hearing about this dance and not witnessing the curious bustle, I was at a loss for words, so I shall rely on an eyewitness for a change. How I do wish I had gotten ashore for this spectacle. Beyond the infrequent waltz, my feet took a fancy to walking. Once I danced with Alice on the ship, she graciously forgave me when I stepped upon her petite toes.

Tillie's Tomato Surprise, the first and only silent movie in which Tom would have a role, was released in 1915, to great acclaim. Starring Marie Dressler, the "Mirth of a Nation" according to advertisements, was full of comedy, clever film shots, and stunts. Marie did her own risky stunts.

Phunster, ever a quality Heathen and solid British citizen, enlisted in the English army in June 1916. The English counsel in New York informed him that they were not taking forty-year-olds no matter how funny they were. Part of the reason for his enlistment was his stepping upon Hungarian star Mitzi Hajos's toes in a scene from their Broadway show *Pom-Pom*. Not speaking much English, Mitzi, after the curtain fell, pitched into Tom with an avalanche of American cuss and slang words. At the end of the mangled verbal barrage, Tom simply replied, "Well, I must say, Mitzi, you are getting on in your English. Where did you learn all that stuff?" Proudly, Mitzi replied, "I pick 'im oop from ze stagehands."

In September 1920, while performing in the play *Magic Melody* in Syracuse, New York, Phunster had a nervous breakdown. Little Mother immediately took him to England and placed him in a sanitarium to recuperate for several weeks, his mind was a blank. She then cared for him at home until he was fully recovered. An undisclosed illness was diagnosed, yet he was discharged from the hospital after beating the one in one thousand odds placed against him for survival in 1921. He returned to the stage, and the ailment overwhelmed him again. Our beloved Tom McNaughton, who had provided us with so much great entertainment, died in 1923. Happening upon his isolated obituary in the provincial *Derby Telegraph* on the very bottom of page six, I thought

Tom would be amused by its proximity and brevity to the notice printed immediately above his obituary. Forever regulated to the provinces, so it seemed.

A sparrow hawk, entering the house of a bird fancier of Barrow-In-Furness,
Swooped down on a linnets cage but was killed with a stick before it could
Reach the linnet. (a small finch with a fondness for hemp)
Mr Tom McNaughton, the survivor of the Brothers McNaughton,
The comedian's, died last evening in the nursing home at St Albans.

Tom did do much better while alive, when he was billed in his role of Percy Jitney in the movie "Tillie's Tomato Surprise" right above James the Monkey.

Alice's lonesome newspaper obituary in 1949 from Winnipeg, Canada, showed how she had been relegated to almost complete obscurity.

BONNIE BELLE DIES; Barnstead, Surry, England. Alice Lloyd. 76, comedienne
Known as the "Bonnie Belle of Scotland" died in her home Thursday.
She was the sister of Marie Lloyd, brilliant English and Pantomime artist.

Most of us are condemned to the forgetfulness of each passing generation. Acknowledged as a symbol of an era in America, her death notice was barely a printed whisper for such an accomplished talent. A mere thimble full of ink in contrast to the many gallons devoted to her articles in newspapers past. The girl that made the name Lloyd a household word in America was neglected in England, yet still, Alice wanted to write her sister Marie's story in 1922.

ALICE LLOYD

ONE OF THE THREE GREATEST BOX OFFICE RECORD BREAKERS IN THE WORLD.
—*Harrisburg Daily Independent*, 4 December 1911

Miss Lloyd could draw an entire bill of headliners bushed together.
—Oscar Hammerstein, 1914

In 1949, her friends at *Variety* magazine afforded ample ink and devoted one-third of a page as a retrospect of her twenty-five-year career, a rarity for them. She and Tom had placed hundreds of quarter-and-half-page advertisements in that magazine to announce new shows, extend Christmas wishes, and thank their many loyal patrons since its inception in 1905. The increasing prosperity of *Variety* and Alice Lloyd were intertwined.

I think prohibition is a jolly good thing for the theater.
People will naturally the seek
the Vaudeville House when the saloon doors are closed to them.
—Alice Lloyd, *New-York Tribune*, 7 December 1919

"The delightful Dresden doll delineator of delightful ditties," Sime wrote on 4 July 1908. I only saw her sing once, on our ship in the midst of a hurricane. She brought calm to a room undulating from the waves. One could not imagine such genuine emotion coming from the dainty lady, but it radiated throughout the café. Her bold fearlessness inspired a rare confidence that touched all within the sound of her voice.

Maybe not the talent of enduring greatness for which others are remembered, but humanity chose to slight Alice Lloyd. Dr. Jones found it incomprehensible that in her obituary she was accorded secondary status to her sister Marie. Marie might have won the hearts of the English people, but Alice conquered the rest of the English-speaking world. Two decades of headlines, packed houses, and standing lines to get into theaters proved that she was more admired and more accomplished than her "brilliant" sibling. Alice was conferred a great honor when she became the first female life member of the White Rats of America. To her children, she was an exceptional mother. Alice was the kind of gal that needed no affirmation other than witnessing the happiness of her children and seeing the enjoyment upon the faces of her audiences calling for encore after encore of "Splash Me."

> October 1st Montreal, Canada. After an absence of 4 years From the vaudeville stage, Alice Lloyd appeared here yesterday Before a capacity audience and received the heaviest ovation Ever tendered a vaudevillian in this city.
>
> *Variety*, October 3rd,1919

Homeward: New York to Liverpool, Day II

By now, you may have noticed that some of the Heathen women would not have the longest acting careers, but were definitely the most physically attractive. In 1913, anyone who has seen Dai Turgeon as Mme. De Claux in the *Girl from Montmarte* at the Grand Opera House in NYC would attest to this fact. On 3 October, Dai (SISTER SUNNY) was welcomed into the pagan realm along with William Boosey (BROTHER BILLY). Mr. Boosey was the managing director of Messrs. Chappell & Co. music publishers in England. In addition, he produced concerts and plays and was a director of the Lyric Theater and Queen's Hall. Everyone noticed that the fifty-five-year-old Billy was indeed taken with the barely eighteen-year-old Dai (her not being shy and playfully seductive), going so far as to write "We were married before we knew each other"—how déjà vu. If Sister Sunny was inspired, she failed to show it, but she added a poem that brought a tear to the old doc's eye.

Little Dai so bright and spry
How she hates to say goodbye
See her wipe each straining eye
When she bids the Chief goodbye [and the orchestra?].

Unannounced to the assembled profane this night ,Sister Sunny was discreetly undertaking an enforced excursion. The French-Canadian lady's task was "to divert her mind from matrimony". Her father Charles, it seems, was not overjoyed by her two year romance with 48 year old, former Yale Football captain, Charles Belmont Davis. Mr

Davis's appointment as consul to Florence,Italy, in 1893 by President Cleveland, bore scant credence when concerning his tender daughter. Outwardly, judging by her gusto, the Big Chief surmised Little Dai to be well versed.

Two months later Charles Davis arrived in London, found his beloved had gone to Paris with friends for the New Year, and, never unpacking, crossed the channel. Two weeks later,on January 17th, the reunited couple were back in London exchanging vows at St James Church.

The newlyweds enjoyed their honeymoon at a castle, in the resort town of Frinton- on-Sea, courtesy of his brother Richard Harding Davis, the famous writer and war correspondent. Richard shared his brothers proclivity for actresses, marrying Bessie McCoy, the dazzling Yama- Yama girl, the preeminent actress Ethel Barrymore was their maiden of honor. Pauline Ada, Dai, never acted again, returning to America to become a assertive socialite and spiritualist after the sudden death of brother-in law Richard in 1916.

Her husband, Charles, penned several books. Curiously, his first, entitled *The Stage Door,* in 1908, was clearly based upon personal experience. His writings included many magazine articles and several movies. *Nothing a Year*, published in 1916, portrayed the story of an unprincipled and ambitious young girl who condemned the morals and manners of New York society. The Davis's brother's talents originated from literary pedigree, their mother was the famous Rebecca Harding Davis.

Pirates are rarely a concern to us on the *Maury*. To Brother Billy, they were his nemesis. He resoundingly believed that these musical pirates not only stole revenue from the artists but threatened to annihilate musical copyright altogether. In 1902, he led the organizing of the Musical Defense League. The only recourse for the artist or publisher, at this time, was in civil court, where the convicted defendant paid the imposed fine. When the offender left trial they would immediately begin printing more counterfeit copies. As Mr. Boosey pointed out, popular music only required two or three pages of paper, and they could be photographed or lithoed in any "old shed or barn that happened to be handy." The sheets were then retailed by an army of street hawkers for distribution. By 1905 the situation had worsened, even to the point of books being printed illegally. The increased printing of music finally convinced the Music Publishers Association to proclaim, in the *Daily*

Telegraph, that there would be "no further musical publications, no fresh contracts, and no further money spent on newspaper ads." The industry was at a standstill. In 1906 a new law was quickly passed, making it a criminal offense to pirate music. That was sweet music for musicians and publishers, but did not affect my tone-deaf ears.

Brother Billy always made news—he was an affable gentleman. In 1916, with only three weeks to campaign, he ran a last-minute effort to be elected to Parliament in the Tewkesbury division, a rural constituency that covered hundreds of square miles. Mounting a vigorous and energetic effort, he realized on Election Day that it would be difficult to defeat seventy-five-year-old William Hicks-Beach (who only served until 1918). In those days autos were employed to ferry voters to the polling booths. Hicks-Beach had 360 cars at his disposal, while Mr. Boosey deployed only six. "It makes one smile when one realizes you may petition to unseat a successful candidate if hired cars are used to bring up electors to the polling booths," William wrote. With so few cars, he did manage 1,438 votes to his opponent's 7,127. By my calculations he was only 354 cars from being elected.

Homeward: New York to Liverpool, Day V

The new 1914 year commenced in a most queer demeanor. When the barometer dropped, it did not forecast the violent storms of the prior year. "Smooth seas do not make good sailors," or so the African proverb goes. The travelers behaved more subdued than we were normally accustomed. *If it's not the weather and it's not the seas, then what to attribute the sedate mood on board* the surgeon wondered.

The ship departed Liverpool for New York, and acolytes were sparse. In fact, no feasts had occurred until the night of March 22, and then we had few in number on that final night of the voyage. Maybe the mood changed because the Irish members of the crew added caring for the seventeen thousand shamrock plants in the cargo hold to their duties. What would St. Patrick's Day be like in New York without shamrock plants!

On the brink of abandoning all hope for this crossing, I received heartening responses for the ritualistic evening meal from Paul and Elsa Friedman from New Orleans. Paul was a broker. Surprisingly, Julie Opp

Faversham accepted an invite, and the farewell party was scheduled. Mrs. Faversham was heading to England, I had read that she had been ill and had taken six months off the stage, but appeared" in the pink" to me at dinner. She and her husband, actor William Faversham, had just completed a short engagement at the Lyric Theater in New York, presenting and starring in the play *Othello*, co-starring our own Constance Collier. Miss Opp had confidential business in England.

> There is a new sex coming, it will be a Portia-like man/women. The new women will have a mind as highly developed as any man without losing any of that delicacy and tenderness of her sex which lends so maternally to her charm. It will take centuries for the complete evolution, but the final outcome is inevitable. Man has feminized her too much and crammed her into a mold.
>
> —Julie Opp, 1913

Julie Opp was an enchanting woman. Daughter of Bowery innkeeper and local political figure Johnny Opp, she went to London after his passing. Convent educated, the sisters remonstrated the young eight-year-old Julie when she was discovered in the chapel acting out the death scene of *Camille*, replete with gurgling and choking! Miss Opp began her career as a journalist writing magazine articles. Sarah Bernhardt, after being interviewed by Julie, persuaded her to try acting and giving her a role as an extra in her production of *Camille* when the show moved to London. She merely had five French words as a speaking line: "Comment se-vat ill, Marguerite." George Alexander gave her the role as Julia Neilson's understudy in *As You Like It*. When Miss Neilson became ill, Julia stepped into the role and, as they say in the theater, was discovered.

Blessed with superb height, a pretty face, and a charming manner, she soon won the hearts of her audiences and actor Robert Lorraine, who, at that time, was the most handsome actor on the British stage. In 1897, they married in London the day before sailing to New York. The courtship lasted longer than the marriage. Julie was quoted saying "it lasted only one night and one day," but legally a year. Robert Lorraine was caught registering with his wife in the Rossmore Hotel in New York the same night Julie was onstage in Bridgeport, Connecticut.

Less than a year later, in 1902, she was engaged and married to Mr. Faversham, while being pursued by playwright Justin McCarthy, who had dedicated a play, *If I Were King*, to Julie. On stage Julie's talents were flourishing on both sides of the Atlantic (mostly in England), she managed to find time to publish a novel entitled *The Squaw Man* in 1906, adapted from the original 1905 Edwin Royle play and, later, a movie. She would again be sickened with tuberculosis in late March 1914 and went to take the cure in Arosa, Switzerland. This is the trip where she favored us at the Heathen table. Whereas she looked well, even I, the good doctor, did not know we were ferrying Julie to Europe for medical treatments. In May, her husband and two boys would reunite there with her and spend some time in Lake Lucerne.

In July 1914, she and Mr. Faversham were headed back to America on the *Olympic*. Mrs. Evelyn Thaw's stateroom was directly across Mrs. Stanford White's. In 1908, Mrs. Thaw's jealously deranged but wealthy husband Harry had shot Mr. White to death at a rooftop theater in New York. Annoyed by the propinquity of her deceased husband's former lover, Mrs. White wanted but could not find other accommodations. When Stanford died, his architect partner Charles Mckim would become very close to Mrs. White. Charles would be stricken with heart trouble while staying at the widowed wife's home in Providence, Rhode Island, in 1909. Mckim died days later. Evelyn refused to change staterooms. Hearing of the predicament, Mr. and Mrs. Faversham exchanged rooms with Mrs. White. To Miss Opp's perseverance, November would find her in Carnegie Hall—not for acting but to put forth a suffrage resolution.

After retreating to her New York home in Huntington, on the north shore of Long Island in 1916 to recuperate and rest again, she would appear infrequently at social affairs, but made an effort for Red Cross and war relief events. High Priestess Constance Collier noted in her book what great parties the Faversham's had at their home in England. In April 1921, ravaged by TB, she died after an operation at the Postgraduate Hospital in Manhattan. Her husband, William, rushed home from acting in Ohio when he learned his wife's condition had worsened. A bright light, toward which all Heathens navigate, was extinguished on the horizon.

A chill went up and down my spine as it did many others en route Friday night, the twenty-second of May 1914. Five hundred miles southeast of Cape Race, the topmast lookout sighted an iceberg. A hard-to-port order was swiftly issued, and the ship veered sharply, narrowly missing the migrant berg. Two additional growlers (small icebergs) were sighted. Days later Cunard disputed the closeness of the iceberg, but those on board knew it to be closer than the company led you to imagine. Immediately I wondered how well the frigidometer was working.

Homeward: New York to Liverpool, Day IV

Nights, when I sit at the table for initiations, I mulled over, *Why so many actresses?* First, they said yes to the invitations. Second, they were attractive and youthful. Most importantly, they were great fun. 30 May was the night. As my eyes circumnavigated the table and the assembled dramatis personae, I came to the conclusion we had enough actors and writers to do our own play that night, should we be tasked. I really could play a doctor. Margret Mayo Selwyn (SISTER BABY MINE), writer and actor; her husband, actor Edgar Selwyn (BROTHER NASTY TERRIER); Leslie Faber (BLACK CORA); and Holbrook Blinn (ANY OLD KNIGHT LSD), who had just finished a play in Chicago with his wife, Ruth Benson Blinn (OFFICIAL TERRAPLIN), were on one side. The other side was occupied by H. Nye Chart (LOOK OUT PEEPS), Leonore Harris (SISTER PATSY, her mark, the whip) looking lovely, LITTLE CHIEF (Arthur Pearse), and myself, BIG CHIEF not so lovely.

First order of business was raising Sister Patsy to the Order of the Yellow Ribbon for her conspicuous chastity. She had just completed 163 performances in the play *The Whip* at the Manhattan Opera House and was heading to Europe for an extended tour in the role of Mrs. D'Aquila. Miss Harris would write a book for her nursery aged child in 1943, about the family's Great Dane entitled *The Big Lonely Dog.* She would have a bad experience in Germany as she, Alice Lloyd, and Tom McNaughton, would be in the wrong country when war broke out.

Leonore would be caught ten kilometers from the fighting in the town of Metz, where her troupe was performing. At first, she was treated terribly by the Germans, her luggage was confiscated, and her money was appropriated. She was forcibly put on a train to Switzerland, and the trip took seventy hours as there was much damage to the tracks, which caused constant delays. Fortunately, she had trustable checks that enabled her to pay for passage. The raven-haired actress was most often cast as the seductive villainess, which might have helped her foil the Germans.

Portions of the conversation this evening were out of the realm of your obligatory doctor, but I will disclose them for your edification. It began with the term *pit*, in reference to theater. When the original Drury Lane Theater was built in 1663, the ground floor was styled the "Pit", because that exact spot was where cockfights had regularly taken place during the reign of James I. The terms *sock and buskin* were used by the theater crowd, which literally means "comedy and tragedy." A *soccus* was a low shoe worn by the ancient actors. An alternative shoe worn by the ancients, the bursa, reached to the knee extending the actor's height. Imprisoned table-side by these actors, they next discussed *deadhead*, which aroused my curiosity. In 1850s, the principal avenue of Detroit had a tollgate close to the entrance of the Elwood Cemetery road. As the cemetery had been laid out before the construction of the plank road, it was ordained that all funeral processions should pass for free. One day, Dr. Pierce, an important local physician, stopped to pay his toll and queried the gatekeeper, "Considering the benevolent nature of our profession, you ought to let us pass free of charge." "No, no, Doctor," replied the man, "we can't afford that. We send too many deadheads through here as it is." Who says the 2:00 a.m. conversations of actors are boring? Medical inquiry concerning the final story kept my sore sleepy gluteus maximus adhered to the chair.

Top picture left to right. At the top: “Leslie Faber” “Leonore Harris” “Arthur Pearse” “Eva Kern” “Holbrook Blinn”
Middle: “Margaret Mayo” “Ruth Benson” sitting
“Edgar Selwyn” “H Nye Chart”
Bottom picture, top left to right: “Leslie Faber” “Leonore Harris” “Arthur Pearse” “Jerome Kern” “Holbrook Blinn” “Ruth Benson”
Bottom right: “H Nye Chart”

HEATHER NOVITIATES.

MAY 30.

Margaret Mayo. Selwyn (Sister Babyhood) 631.

Eleanor Harris (Sister Patsy) 632.

Edgar Selwyn (Brother Nearly Married) 633.

Leslie Faber (B. Uncle Cora) 634.

H. Nye Chart (Look Out) Rep. 635.

(31st). Holbrook Blinn (Anyoldnight) L.S.d. 636.

HEATHENS PRESENT.

Big Chief (his mark).

Little Chief

Officine Terraplin

A popular but now forgotten actor was H. Nye Chart, whom we welcomed to the clan. Fresh from acting alongside fellow initiate Leslie Faber in *Romance*, the play at the Majestic Theater in New York, to good reviews. He was the son of Henry and Ellen Nye Chart, owners of the Theater Royal in Brighton, England, one of the leading provincial theaters in England. Additionally, he had written several family musical comedies for the British stage (pantomimes), most notably *Aladdin* in 1893. Currently, he was happily married to actress Violet Raye. He would act alongside Kathyrn Tyndall and Holbrook Blinn. Lookout would have a long and well-regarded career.

Margret Mayo wrote these fine words in the Heathens' honor:

So may the tribe increase of this good Heathen gang
In every line may all their praise be sang
Tis easy work to score the failures, sneer at everything
But only brave hearts cheer the passing friend
So may true friendship gauge the password of the Heathen tribe
Sans rage.

30 May 1914

Margaret is a long-forgotten celebrity from the beginning of the last century, a tiny, petite, spirituel young lady who mastered the art of the farce in words. She wrote *Baby Mine*, which achieved great recognition, first as a book then a movie, not to mention the three hundred thousand dollars in royalties in one year. She followed that success with other books, *Polly of the Circus* and *Twin Beds*, both of which were made into movies. All were far more popular than her first book, *Our Fate and the Zodiac*, which she published in 1901.

Miss Mayo took an extended trip to the South Sea Islands to make a prolonged study of the domestic culture of the natives. She disclosed that "every baby was deemed the responsibility of every mother, regardless of parents, and every father was responsible for support. No hint or the taint of illegitimacy changed that outlook. And yet we call them savages". This research comprised the basis of her hugely popular book and play *Baby Mine*.

She became a master of self-promotion in an era when women were attempting to get the vote and break the bonds of the male-dominated world. I espied two stories worthy of limited amusement. Miss Mayo lost her dog, a hairless Mexican terrier named "Yet". Gifted by the Mexican minister to the United States, Senor Romero, the errant canine was valued at one million dollars. These terriers were sacred to the Aztecs, as companions and food, and when "Yet", the dog, was lost, Margaret offered a one-hundred-dollar reward. Hundreds of dogs were brought to her apartment, but none were "Yet" Of significance to me was that Margaret, along with Edgar Selwyn, would be two of the first actors to visit Europe in WWI. They entertained the troops in France in the volunteer units of the YMCA show *Over There.* The book of her wartime experiences was entitled *Trooping for the Troops*. C'est la guerre.

The second story was overly publicized and followed in the papers. Margaret made a one-hundred-dollar wager with a producer that she could write an entire play in twenty-four hours. After her Saturday night appearance in a play, she went home and, at 2:00 a.m., began dictating to Theodore Bert Sayre, her stenographer. Eighteen hours and sixteen thousand words later, *The Mart* was conceived. A tale of intrigue, it involved a copper broker, a wife, a mistress, and shady business dealings. I do not think it ever made it to the stage, but she gained plenty of newspaper coverage.

In 1901, Edgar and Margaret were performing onstage in Buffalo, New York. The well attended play was entitled *Arizona*. The two leading actors mimicked their roles in real life, and at the conclusion of the play's final Buffalo performance, they scampered to Niagara Falls to be married. It would be the beginning of a long and successful collaboration between them. He would soon produce the widely applauded *Squaw Man* and begin a long career in films (Edgar was the *wyn* in Goldwyn Pictures in 1916). After 18 years of harmony she divorced Edgar in Reno in 1919, desertion was the charge, but other stories suggested there was discord at the studio.

> "Women must be lacking a sense of humor; or why in the world would they ever take men seriously".
>
> Mme Germaine DeStael, 1800

Edgar had a ticket on the *Titanic*, but a commitment to hear a reading of a new play in London prevented his departure. The Potamides would smile a second time upon him. In 1892, in Chicago, the seventeen-year-old Edgar, his parents recently deceased, penniless and forlorn, decided to commit suicide. He jumped off a bridge spanning the Chicago River and landed on the ice. Instead of drowning as planned, bewildered by his predicament, he reconsidered, and walked back to shore. Lurking in the shadows was a robber with a gun. "Your money or your life," the thief said, to which Mr. Selwyn replied, "My life." The befuddled mugger changed his mind. The two desperate men began a conversation, took the gun to a nearby pawnshop, split the proceeds, and went to breakfast. Now that is a fine example of successful negotiation. This encounter would be the basis for Edgar's 1915 play *Rolling Stones*.

Leslie Faber was the husband of our very own esteemed actress Winifred Arthur Jones Faber (SISTER PEGGY). Together, they raised a daughter, Jean, with the most graceful middle name, Virtue. Tall and handsome, he was a very appealing, well-regarded, and amply-paid actor for the first three decades of the 1900s, mostly in America before the war. October would find him acting in the New York revival of the play *Diplomacy*. An avid sailor, he owned and captained a first rate ten-ton sailboat named *Chiquita*.

In June 1915, Mr. Faber was acting in the play *The White Feather* in New York. The tale was about courage. During the war, British women passed out white feathers as a symbol of cowardice to able-bodied men in England. First, he found out that his wife, at the last minute, had decided not to sail on the torpedoed *Lusitania*. Then, as art imitates life, he immediately left the play and returned to England to be gazetted into the army's Machine Gun Corps as a second lieutenant. In July 1917, he was awarded the Victoria Cross for bravery in action, reportedly keeping his machine gun operating after his entire squad had been killed in spite of intense, hostile fire at Vimy Ridge. His brave actions resulted in a promotion to major. It was written that his men liked and respected him and enjoyed his sense of humor in trying circumstances. In early April 1918 he was reported killed in action during a battle at Picardy. Believed to be missing in May, in June, the Red Cross insisted he was a German prisoner.

Between battles, Mr. Faber found time to entertain his fellow troops at the front, being joined by Lillian Braithwaite in *The Gowl*, written by his father-in-law, Henry Arthur Jones. Happily he resumed his acting career in April 1919 in the Japanese tragic play *The Faithful*, playing the role of a captain in the heroine Kira's guard. Not sure how he took the demotion. Later, he divorced Winifred Jones Faber to marry actress Gladys Grey. In 1929, he was stricken onstage while performing *By Candlelight*, dying two weeks later from heart failure brought on by pleurisy and pneumonia. The most gallant of the Heathens.

The righteous Reverend Dr. George Houghton's Little Church around the Corner in New York was the most irrefutable marrying place in the country. Known to its regular parishioners as the Church of the Transfiguration, it was located on Twenty-Ninth Street between Madison and Fifth Avenue. Many years ago actors could not receive a funeral service and were refused burial at most churches in America. The reasoning was that the occupation of being a follower of Thespis attracted many unsavory and nonspiritual (godless) creatures into that profession. In 1895 famous American actor Joseph Jefferson was refused a funeral service for his departed acting friend George Holland by the pastor of one of New York's most prominent places of worship. He said to Mr. Jefferson, "Funeral services for theatrical people are never held in this church, but there is a little church around the corner where services can be held." "Thank God for the little church around the corner," Mr. Jefferson exclaimed. Whether married or buried, so began a theatrical legend.

So it should not be a complete surprise that one afternoon in August 1896, while rehearsing for a play in New York, Holbrook Blinn and his adored soubrette, co-star Ruth Benson, gathered the entire company and trooped over to the Little Church to get married. It would be a love that would last. Ruth was a pretty, petite Hawaiian brunette. A former schoolteacher fluent in several languages, she became enamored with the stage in 1892, much to the chagrin of her parents, US Army major Henry and Mrs. Benson.

Holbrook's (Any Old Knight L S D) popularity was on the rise. His 1920 role as Pancho Lopez in the play *The Bad Man* would make him a star. In 1914, he was beginning his movie career, where his co-stars would be Marion Davies, Mary Pickford, Minnie Maddern Fiske, and W. C. Fields. Long recognized as one of the premier actors on the English-speaking stage, he was an avid tennis player and accomplished polo player. In 1905, Mr. Blinn would hear the call of the patriarchal redwoods in the Bohemian Grove, where all good bohemians go for idolization, fraternization, and revitalization. Mr. Blinn never saw a stage so rustic.

Evidently, after playing Napoleon in the *Duchess of Dantzic* in 1906, he began collecting artifacts of the deceased dictator and amassed a museum-worthy collection. He and Ruth would act onstage for many years together and he would become both director and a producer. In 1928, while I was serving on the *Aquitania*, I read that Mr. Blinn fell from his horse, injuring his arm. It became infected, and after a failed blood transfusion, the infection worsened. He died in the arms of his beloved Ruth. He was buried on their splendid farm overlooking the Hudson River, fittingly named Journey's End.

Homeward: New York to Liverpool, Day V

On 31 May 1914, the seas were much calmer than the events in Europe. Unheralded to us, the young Bosnians and the Black Hand were about to change the path of history. Their goal, a Serbian-led united Slavic state, to be named Yugoslavia. They would succeed. Our disparate group gathered quality draftees: Roland N. Moore (BROTHER TERPS); Francis Palmer (SISTER BISQUIT), an interior designer on her way to Paris; and timber agent C. Norman Coupland (BROTHER JAM POT), who was always looking for pine around the world. Brother Terps was an art dealer, like his father, Rufus, before him—not just any dealer but one of the most respected antique collectors in the world. (Roland and Rufus traveled more than I did.) Rufus was reputed to have had the most complete Oriental art collection in the world. He founded the American Art Gallery. Roland would inherit the galleries in London and New York when his father died in 1918 and continue the family business.

Eva Kern (SISTER BLONDIE) and her husband, a famous composer, Jerome Kern (BROTHER LAUGHING HUSBAND), made the evening the cause célèbre. In 1909, on one of his many previous trips to England, Mr. Kern had taken a river cruise with friends and happened to dock at the Swan Inn at Walton on the Thames River, owned by Eva's father. In love at first sight, the yearning Jerome hurriedly married the beguiling nineteen-year-old Eva Leale. I will not recount the accomplished musician's storied career on these pages, but it was prolific and enduring. He never needed anyone to put the finishing touches on his musical scores. Once, he told an admirer, "The fact that the theatergoing public likes my music is no credit to me. There are many other composers who write better music that the public doesn't like." He might have written the songs for *Show Boat* and owned a boat named that, but wasn't one. Poker playing and a hangover induced Mr Kern to miss one boat, the sailing of the Lusitania from Pier 54, 1 May 1915.

When the waves are less than ten feet, the sea is calming to most people, but not to one fair but inwardly disturbed young Swedish lass. Eina Spiik was escorting her younger brother, Helge, to America, who wanted to make his fortune. She had previously spent time in Washington, DC, with her older brother, Charles, a banker. Yielding to his sister's pleas, Charles left the job and took the homesick girl back to Sweden. The younger brother decided to take his turn. Surrendering to his pleadings, she agreed to escort him to America.

Miss Spiik spent two days brooding at the stern rail after departing Liverpool. On 13 June, just as Helge was coming to take her to lunch, she grabbed his arms, kissed him, and said, "Good-bye, Helge dear," and suddenly, the pensively distraught girl threw herself over the rail into the black ocean. Passengers' who are restraining suicidal tendencies find the vastness of the sea and sky agitates a strange reaction, compelling them to do what our poor Eina did.

Upon hearing the alarm, Commander J. T. Charles turned the ship around and circled the area where the girl jumped. A small boat was lowered, and they searched for an hour. The forlorn girl's body was never recovered. Once in a while the doctor's medicine bag has no remedy for what ails the mind or heart.

Homeward: New York to Liverpool, Day II

Recruitment was truly a study in contrasts. Many, none, and, sparingly, only had the madcap. The night of 18 June 1914 was the latter. It was actress night, though. Kathyrn Tyndall (SISTER BEAUTY) and Alice Gale (SISTER 55) joined BIG CHIEF and SISTER LIZ. Philadelphia native Alice Gale was a very popular and prominent character actress, having toured the entire United States and Canada. She had just completed a 280-performance run at the Forty-Eighth Street Theater in New York in the play *Today*. In 1916, when

Today was made into a movie, Alice was joined on the movie set with Leonore Harris (Eve), her confiscated luggage amazingly returned by the Germans.

The year 1886 found her in the controversial play *Yorick's Love* in New York. The year 1890 found her in *Wages of Sin* and, later in the year, winning the starring role of Portia in the *Merchant of Venice* alongside the great American actor Edwin Booth. Alice professed that "Shakespeare does not pay. His plays do not yield the kind of returns that other lines of drama, infinitely less worthy, do." She added that she would be "going into a more modern school of acting and would bid a weeping farewell to the Bard of Avon."

In 1916, after forty years on the stage, she would make her first film. She would get most favorable reviews for the 1918 film *Birth of Race*, calling her acting some of the finest ever produced on a screen. Sister 55 had a long career onstage and on-screen, well known, and beloved by her audiences. There was an amusing story overheard by Sister 55, as told to the assembled druids. Walking home from the theater after a performance, she overheard a poor woman talking to a doctor, saying to him, "I suppose yer getting a pretty good fee for attending that rich Valentine boy?"

"Of course, I'll be getting a good fee, but why do you ask?"

"Because," said the woman, "I don't want you to forget that it was my boy Martin that threw the brick that hit him, and I expect a commission."

Sister Beauty, Kathryn Tyndall was on the way to join a traveling troupe, to play the lead in a new presentation of the play *The Yellow Ticket*. Dramatist Michael Morton's play tells the story of a woman who wants to see her dying father, but since she is Jewish and living in czarist Russia, she is restricted to living within her own village. When she finds out prostitutes can travel freely by obtaining a yellow ticket, she degrades herself to qualify and leaves to seek her father (she does not know he is already dead). It would be a long-running play and well attended. Kathryn was an acclaimed leading lady in Broadway's David Belasco Company. Alfred Dryer would be very fortuitous, in 1916, to marry Miss Tyndall in New York, New York. The red-flaxen-haired Kathryn would become a famous acting and voice coach and teacher with a virtual who's who of clients from stage, screen, radio, and opera. She offered night classes to those who had dreams and little money. In

1941, as another war began, she said, "Right is truth, and truth shall never be swallowed by might."

The Heathen Anthem
By Kathryn Tyndall

My great chief's a doctor, now what do you think of that,
He wears gold braided jackets, a little gold lame cap
He wore a blooming choker, around his bleeding heart,
Now my great chief's a doctor, on a Cunard steamship boat.

Homeward: New York to Liverpool Day I

On the seventh day of July, the ship barely fifty miles from the dock, someone procured the treasured archive. Its appropriation remains a mystery to the chronicler, and by whom, is quite another matter. If one is to borrow the sacred text to do foulness upon its pages, it would be most sacrilegious, and I am happy to report that is not the case. Mr. Leo Carrillo, former cartoonist for the *San Francisco Examiner* and *Variety* magazine, graced us with a full-page drawing.

Leo was becoming known as a vaudevillian actor and, later, a movie star, you will best know him as the Cisco Kid's partner, Pancho. His first stage appearance was an accident. While in the audience at the San Frisco Orpheum Theater, the headliner canceled, and Lee was reluctantly pressed into service. He was not booed off the stage. The show caught-on and management extended the engagement.

Leo was returning to England with his wife, Marie, to headline at the King's Theater as "the scholarly monologist with the dialect stories galore." Not in Mr. Carrillo's wildest dreams did he imagine at this moment that theatrical producer Oliver Morosco would see his vaudeville act. Witnessing Leo's performance and recognizing a budding talent, Morosco offered him a part of the French valet in his upcoming play *Upstairs and Downstairs* in 1916. After great success in that role, he was cast as the leading man in *Lombardi Ltd.* And 296 performances later, Leo was a star.

The future movie star dedicated the drawing to me, and I am not sure if I am to be grateful or not. It has a sketch of the *Mauretania* at a 45 percent angle being ridden by a Chinese man standing on the stern, saying, “Me heap likee *Mauretanee.* It go like hellee.” Why he worried about a sinking ship when he was an excellent swimmer, I cannot fathom. Mr. Carrillo often used the Chinese character and dialect in his vaudeville act. The well-drawn cartoon was accepted graciously, but I was still pondering its meaning. Noteworthy, the portion of the bow out of the water has a sizeable chink in it.

Mr. Carrillo's sketch of the *Maury* with a hole in its bow and sinking by the stern was not that unlikely. On the night of 5 August 1914 at 11:30 p.m., our ship was off Sable Island in the North Atlantic. Our ship received a wireless from the British cruiser HMS *Essex* advising to immediately change course to Halifax Harbour rather than continue toward New York because German warships were sighted nearby, twenty miles and closing. The crew was informed, but the passengers were not told of the declaration of war. They knew something was amiss when the ship suddenly, and without warning, changed course and increased its speed noticeably. The portholes were draped with canvas (and those on the starboard) blacking out all outside lights. Passengers were informed that it was to keep the rain out. Ominously, the ship went dark. All outside doors leading to the decks were locked.

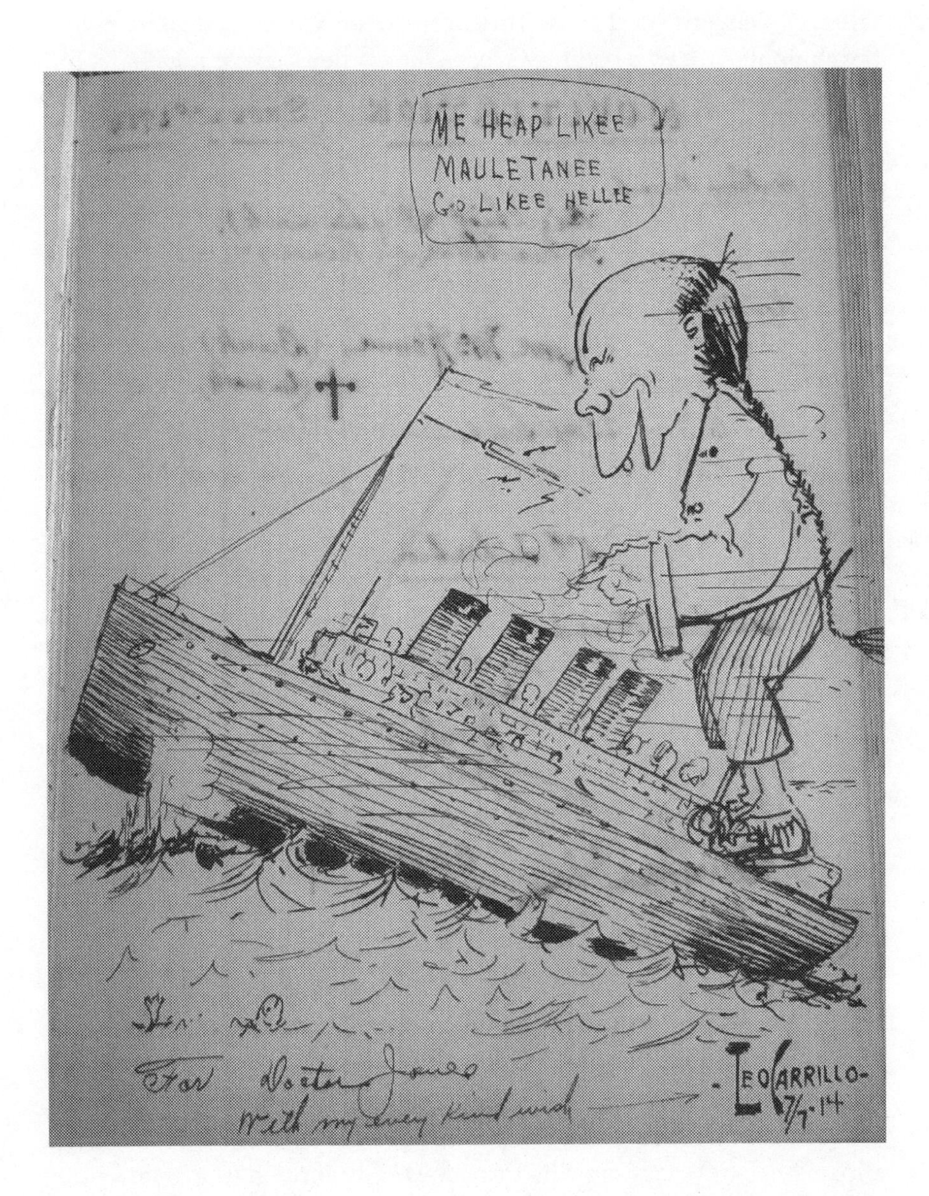
ME HEAP LIKEE
MAULETANEE
GO LIKEE HELLEE
For Doctor Jones
LEO CARRILLO
7/7-14

There was much excitement en route for the next 140 miles and we safely made Halifax in record time at twenty-seven and a half knots. We would later be escorted to New York by a warship. Our sister ship, the *Lusitania*, encountered those three very same German cruisers plying the shipping lanes we had traversed. One of them gave it hot chase, but its speed and the settling of a haze over the water, thwarted her pursuer. The war had come to the *Mauretania*.

The Balkan states are as unfit for self-government
as Turkey. It would be well for humanity if the great
powers assumed the policeman's batan and took
charge of the whole district.
—Herbert Kaufman, *Woman's World*, September 1913

Britain was at war. By August 12, we were formally at war with Austria-Hungary after declaring war on Germany on August 4. The *Mauretania*, now being a ship under direction of the Admiralty, would be pressed into war service. Flying no flag, painted black from stem to stern, armed with six guns on the foredecks, aft decks and amidships, men alert, the *Maury* was now a British warship. On August 19, just as dawn was breaking, the *Mauretania* spotted a ship flying no colors. It swept toward the ship and circled it once. After a brief wireless communication, the ship showed its Dutch colors. It was the passenger ship *Amsterdam*, conveying mostly Americans homeward. The *Mauretania* departed to do more scouting for enemy vessels.

Our return to Liverpool after provisioning in New York on 20 August was unprecedented in Cunard history. We had not one passenger. In the spooky peace within the dining room, the absence of the Heathens' revelry in its dead silence was unsettling.

The Speed Queen of the Atlantic was faster than the U-boats (15 knots) and faster than their torpedoes (26.5 knots). We could do nearly 29 knots for short distances and could average 27.5 with high-grade coal if the need arose. The Maury's massive appetite for coal limited her use as an armed cruiser. We were 2 knots faster than any battleship afloat. The only snag, sighting torpedoes early enough to maneuver out of their direction.

Outbound; Liverpool to New York Day II

War cannot stop a superb soiree. For two month's we were given a reprieve from wartime duty to resume passenger service. Undeterred by the crew on constant alert looking for spies, we managed to secure a good natured menage. The date 2 September was when BIG CHIEF and Anna Taylor (KENSEY) made Thomas Swan Hope Simpson (COPPER), Henry Montague Earle (BUBBLES), and Mayme McKenna (BUNK, her mark, the cross) take the oath. Oom Cum Pivvy Sinkit, hopefully drinks and not the ship.

Thomas Hope Simpson was a world-traveling English merchant representing Balfour, Williamson & Co. in New York. He was very much the athlete, playing cricket and excelling in golf, winning many tournaments with his sister. He was a prominent member of Staten Island Club. His large family included his twin brother, Sir James Hope Simpson, and older brother, John, who was a Member of Parliament in England. Retiring to his 1,500-acre farm in England, Blagroves, to raise purebred Jersey cattle, he would finally reject bachelorhood in 1923 to marry. Tragically, two years later, he would die from heart failure.

Henry Earle (BUBBLES) was a very prominent and well-connected New York and Washington attorney. He was best man at the wedding of US vice president Adlai Stevenson's son, Lewis. A Georgetown Law School graduate, he was involved in several prominent cases during his career. His real avocation was captaining the Squadron A Polo Team. Leading them to victory in many tournaments, he was instrumental in championing the sport in America. Having two passionate sportsmen at the same table is always good for the spectators.

Stealing the show this night was the glamorous Marjorie Mayme McKenna (BUNK), and her moniker was not for a ship's bed. Mayme was the sensational wife of Chicago politician Michael McKenna, close associate of Bathhouse John Coughlin, the Chicago Democratic political leader, and Ward 19 alderman John Powers, "Johnny De Pow." A book could be written about their corruption. They must have been amused at Mayme's about-to-be-related predicament. On previous crossing on our fair vessel in August 1910, she was detained by customs, arrested, and later released into custody of counsel after posting a five-thousand-dollar bond.

Contained within the twelve trunks were found seven Parisian gowns of the latest style worth 1,600 dollars. One cannot imagine how much luggage people brought with them. I think they believed more trunks and hatboxes symbolized more wealth. Microscopically examining the contents, the inspector determined that a Chicago label had been sewn in to replace the Paris tag. In addition, fifteen thousand dollars-worth of jewelry was found. She was arrested for smuggling, a fairly serious crime. Obviously, for years past, the rich smuggling clothing and jewelry, almost carte blanche, to avoid paying import duties, was assumed. Rousting the rich too frequently could be bad for business.

It was exposed that she was traveling not with her husband but rather with Mr. John Powers, her husband's associate. She registered when boarding as Mrs. John Powers of Chicago, as they did later at the New York Waldorf hotel. How convenient to have Mr. Powers on hand after her indictment with bail money. When contacted, the other Mrs. Powers in Chicago denied having been to New York. Further investigation determined that Mr. Powers had paid sixty-five thousand dollars for Mayme's home in Danville, Illinois. Most of the ship's crew wanted to move to Chicago and become alderman since the pay was so good.

In Chicago, one month before she had to appear in New York court, a mysterious fire burnt her 7,500-dollar imported French automobile in its garage at her Michigan Avenue home. Her chauffeur and his wife were forced to jump from the second-story window of the burning building to escape. Firemen never determined the cause of the fire.

Dearest Mother; Robert Adams and
I were quietly married this afternoon.
Please forgive me, your daughter, Pearl

Mayme was stunned in 1905. Her 19 year old daughter had eloped with singer and composer Robert J "Bob' Adams. The man was completely unknown to her. The McKenna Mansion on Michigan Ave held no attraction for the enamored young girl compared to a life on the road with the popular crooner. When Pearl, a freshmen music student at the Chicago Music College, who cared for little except music, heard his song "The Sweetest Girl in Dixie", she was infatuated. Miss McKenna arranged a meeting with him at Saratoga, Mr. Adams lived in NY. After the furtive tryst she moped abaft to the family mansion. St. Patrick's Day, weeks later, after leaving home for the usual music lesson at school, they were married. She became a victim of a Thespian. Three years later, finding a letter which revealed he had an appointment with an unknown girl named "Edith", she was granted a divorce. They reconciled and lived happily in London as Bob played the music halls. He was whistling something that sounded noteworthy. Mayme and daughter toured Europe for some months, often visiting a large estate in France Pearl had fallen heiress to, but were silent about the bequest.

Personally, I posit that Mayme posed as Mrs. McKenna, taking the name of a close political ally of the Chicago gang, Michael "Hinky Dink" Kenna, and really was the permanent mistress of the married Johnny "J. Pow" Powers. In 1918, Johnny married the "widowed" Mrs. Mayme McKenna, alias Mary C. Larrabee, daughter of the former Chicago City treasurer and pioneer hardware retailer. She was worth $250,000., and no ex-husband could be found. BUNK was threatened with prison by the judge after having missed her first court appearance for the smuggling charge. By hook or by crook he found it in his heart to only fine her one thousand dollars and return her five-thousand-dollar bond, which in most cases would have been forfeit. BUNK left off the O.

When next in port, we were painted battleship gray and became a dedicated armed merchant cruiser. I always shook my head in disbelief at how fast the painters could accomplish that feat. At rest, from shore, the ship looked large, menacing, and somber. In September, we secretly conveyed Russian troops from Archangel, Russia, to Aberdeen, Scotland. From there they were conveyed by special trains to the coast of England and then across the channel to Ostend, Belgium. In a pinch, we could transport ten thousand men. So far, the violence of war had ignored us.

Homeward: New York to Liverpool, Day V

Recruiting new initiates was not a problem. Irreverent people find each other, even in troubling times. The night was 14 September. BIG CHIEF had table side Katherine Stuart Burns (KI KI) and Gerald Browne (WHISKEY BEAR). Mr. Browne hailed from Australia and was a civil mining engineer by profession. Two other young ladies were adamant about membership. Older beyond their years I deduced, of legal age they were. I hope their father, Harry, doesn't hear about this episode. The sisters Selfridge, Violette (SISTER LITTLE), twenty years old, and Rosalie (SISTER YUM YUM), twenty one years old, recited the oath, and signed the sacred book. Ki-Ki was employed to tend the young Selfridge girls' behavior and virtue. She succeeded in one of those undertakings.

Violette and Rosalie were amusing and adorable visions of youthful loveliness. On this night I suspected Rosalie would never have imagined that in a few short months she would be a nurse to soldiers in a hospital. Nor did Violette envision distributing rations to incoming trains of wounded men at Charing Cross Station. Their mother, Rosalie, would send 680 personal letters and presents at Christmas to former store employees in the trenches in France. The final archive entry ever to be written was by Rosalie. She wrote, "Sister Yum Yum was this day elected by the above assembled in conclave as *High Sauceress*."

Trailing the Selfridge girls' lives after the war was easy as they often made the newspapers. I found several unexpected similarities. In 1918, Rosalie would marry Serge de Bolotoff, eldest son of Princess Wiasemsky of Russia (with palaces in Petrograd and Moscow!). Serge was employed at the Selfridges' store when he met Rosalie. In 1925, Serge found he would not inherit his family's title or property, which was being appropriated by a surrogate prince. A letter was signed and posted in the newspapers by ten exiled Russian princes living in London who claimed the title for Grand Duke Cyril in the name of the Romanoff's.

Not to be bettered by her older sibling, in 1921, Violette would marry Vicomte Jacques de Sibour—the family had a château in Sollier, France. They would meet on an Atlantic liner (not ours). Soon after, Jacques would take a job in Harry's London store, proving his mettle by hard work, learning the department store business from the bottom-up. Through his arduous labor he proved himself to be worthy of Harry's daughter. Apparently, his serving with distinction as a skillfully decorated pilot in the French Air Force during the war was not enough for Papa Selfridge. Both Heathen-ordained ladies married European royalty. Most peculiar to the Dr. Jones was the youngest Selfridge girl, Beatrice, married Jacques's older brother, Louis de Sibour, pilot and European royalty. Pilots were the swashbuckling young gentlemen of our era. Harry should have bought an airfield.

Rosalie's husband, Serge, was an aeronautical engineer by education who, in 1909, had designed and built his own airplane. In 1913, he built a tri-wing plane at Brooklands Aeroport, one of Britain's first airfields, but only flew it a three times, financing issues, I heard mentioned. Jacques and Violette would, in 1928, begin a honeymoon trip around the world in their little De Havilland Moth plane nicknamed Safari II. Ostensibly to be a pleasurable rather than record setting jaunt, it potentially would be grueling and perilous. Violette recounted their story in her 1930 book *Flying Gypsies*, published by George Putnam, husband of Amelia Earhart.

As a matter of course Jacques and Violette became close friends with the Putnam's. Papa Selfridge had displayed Amelia's plane from her 1932 solo flight across the Atlantic in his London store. Violette was one of the first to send Amelia a cablegram, stating, "Million congratulations. Please come to Paris soon," after Amelia's 1932 solo transatlantic flight. Years later, Violette and the viscount took their two children, son Jean-Jacque and daughter Jacqueline, around the world in their plane. Big Chief would never have imagined the panache that filled of Sister Little.

While employed by the Standard Oil Co. in 1937, Jacques arranged for maps, meteorological reports, gas, supplies, and spare parts along Amelia's around-the-world flight. Amelia called him the good fairy of our flight. He and Violette would last see her in Karachi, India, on her final, bedeviled journey.

Under the umbrella of darkness on, 6 October 1914, we loaded three secret airplanes bound for England, one speculated to be the world's most powerful seaplane named *America*. Recently, the plane had flown at Hammondsport, New York, with ten men, and could lift two thousand pounds. They were to be used by the British government in war service. We had three passengers from the Davison Chemical Co. conveying secret plans for a big gun to counter the German siege gun, the Busy Bertha. Those German guns quickly reduced the fortifications at Liege and Namur to rubble. The guns were so similar many thought the plans had been stolen. We were now munitions runners.

In my later years, I found this worthy of mention. In keeping the family perpetual, Rosalie and Serge's daughter Tatiana would marry Major Craig Smith, who just happened to be the son of Franklin Wheaton-Smith and Ernestine Craig Wheaton-Smith. To put this in Heathen language, SISTER YUM YUM's daughter married the son of PICK AX and SISTER ARIZONA, who was the daughter of KITTEN and FLORA. Maybe, just possibly, Heathen descendants are still roaming the Seven Seas.

"Dulce et Decorum est, pro patria mori."
[It is sweet and lovely to die for one's country.]
—Wilfred Owen

Bidding a fond farewell to New York harbour at the end of October, we were informed we would be refitted as a troop or hospital ship when we returned to Liverpool. *Auxiliary armed cruiser*, *troopship*, *hospital ship*, and *passenger ship* chronicle our participation in the war. After the *Lusitania* was sunk on May 7, all our sailings were temporarily canceled. This article appeared in the newspapers:

Berlin, 13 May 1915

The Mauretania or any other British liner will be
torpedoed, sunk, and
meet the same fate as the Lusitania if our submarines can
reach them.
And that they can has been demonstrated.

In 1915, Heathens Frederick Harrison, Haddon Chambers, Pauline Chase, along with playwright James Barrie and actress Edna May, were instrumental in getting a memorial fountain erected in honor of famous theatrical producer Charles Frohman, who died in the *Lucy*'s torpedoing. The fountain was located at Marlow-on-Thames, Buckinghamshire. When seventy-two-year-old producer Frederick Harrison (Freyda) died 13 June 1926, he bequeathed his entire fortune to his one true love, the Haymarket Theater, rumored to be haunted by actor John Buckstone's phantom, who has become Freyda's best friend.

War stories remain fresh in my enfeebled mind. They are worthy of mention because there was no loss of life shipboard during the war years due to catastrophe or enemy. In 1907, we did lose two stokers, who fell off the gangplank after a night of Thanksgiving celebration, one pulling the other into the icy water with him. Head stoker Hal Kelly jumped in to look for them, but both were lost under the ship. Aside from a few bizarre episodes, we were blessed, but even the goddess Salacia failed to save the ship from the scrappers.

The closest the *Mauretania* ever really came to disaster was in November of 1916, and it was not because of a German submarine. After two years of war, having been fitted and refitted several times from armed merchant cruiser to troopship to hospital ship and back again, the Admiralty was sending us to Canada to pick up more soldiers to replenish all those being lost in battles at the front. We coaled at Liverpool, bunkers filled and coal ports closed successfully, reportedly. Oozing seawater was noticed seeping under the bunker doors two days out to sea. Hours later, it had worsened, and Captain James Charles ordered the ship slowed. The *Mauretania* was listing.

Below deck, the engineers were up to their necks in Atlantic Ocean, which was on the wrong side of the hull. Captain Charles brought the ship around so the listing side faced the breeze, greatly aiding those trying to pump out the water and secure the leaks. The *Mauretania* almost went down, because, after being loaded with coal, unidentified dockworkers failed to screw down the coal port doors on the outside of the ship. Sabotage, which was always a possibility, or plainly negligence?

Actually, we had a much closer call, but mostly unreported. War is such a strange time, is it not? When entirely painted in white with a giant red cross in the center, the Austrian and German subs would surface nearby, look us over, and then respectfully depart. One incident in October 1915 while outfitted as a troopship (making us a legitimate target) under the command of Daniel "Paddy" Dow is memorable.

The *Mauretania* was hugging the coast of Crete in the Ionian Sea, bound for the Gallipoli Peninsula in the Aegean Sea, conveying four thousand troops. Ships will sail closer to shore for safety reasons in wartime. The subs are easier to spot and can only attack from one side effectively (takes a lot of water to conceal a submerged sub). Captain Dow saw the track of the torpedo toward the starboard bow and ordered hard to port. The torpedo missed the ship by five feet, and the Queen of the Cunard fleet came dreadfully close to peril and, perchance, the bottom of the Doric Channel.

Much has been written about the sinking of our sister ship, the immortal *Lusitania*. This story is unfamiliar. In March 1915, while sailing in the Irish Sea under the command of Captain Dow, the ship was flashed a warning from the British Admiralty that a submarine was lying in ambush directly on her course in the Irish Channel. It was the last night of the voyage, and in the lounge, the usual Seamen's Charity Concert was at full gallop. Theater stars Hutin Britton, Nona McAdoo (her father, William, President Wilson's secretary of the treasury), and Elsie Janis were aboard. Captain Dow was requested to lead Miss Janis out onstage for the final act on the program. The captain begged to be excused because of the potential danger of his leaving the bridge at this crucial time. Fearing attack, the Admiralty had ordered him to head straight toward the mouth of the Mersey. Captain Dow's greater fear was that the wireless warning might have been overheard by the U-boat's crew. Captain Dow circled and steered a snaky course to port and safety. Thanks to prescient seamanship, no one found themselves in my kinsman Davy's locker that night.

In April 1915, Captain Dow went on a brief leave of absence precipitated by "nervous" exhaustion and our former Captain Turner retook the *Lucy*'s helm. Fairly remarkable for a boy of thirteen who began his naval career as a deckhand on the sailing ship *White Star*. Captain Turner was happy to be back in command, but found happiness can be unsympathetic.

After the *Lusitania*'s sinking, the Admiralty accused him of not zigzagging after being warned of subs in the area on the fateful day the seventh of May. Inevitably, on New Year's Day 1917, while ferrying Canadian troops to France in command of the SS *Ivernia*, Captain Turner *was* zigzagging and sunk by German torpedoes. Chance was quite capricious with regard to the good Captain.

Collision. You would think there is enough room in the Mediterranean Sea for two ships, however large. It was a moonless night, clear and dark. We were transporting troops bound from Mudros Harbor on Lemnos Island to Naples, Italy. On 24 July 1915, our thirty-three-thousand-ton *Mauretania* collided with the four-thousand-ton *Cardiff Hall* outbound from Malta. Both ships were under direct orders from the Admiralty, and neither vessel was exhibiting lights. There was considerable damage, but culpability was to be determined. The court of inquiry later found neither party negligent.

On 2 May 1917, Cunard Lines denied newspaper reports that the *Mauretania* was sunk by a German submarine. We were constantly defying the U-boat blockade of England, and very successfully, I might add.

In 1917, Simon Lake, the inventor of the keel-laid submarine, successfully raised ten million dollars to build a four-hundred-feet-long

Sub-Mauratania, a giant undersea merchant vessel that could carry eight thousand tons!

Imagine you are standing at Battery Park in Brooklyn in 1918. It is 7:40 p.m. A great crowd has gathered, braving a drizzly 2 December wind that chills to the bone. Looking out toward Gravesend Bay you see a dazzle-painted huge blue-black-and-white checkerboard-style ship. Her decks covered with four thousand khaki-clad soldiers. The ships guns at rest, her flags are fluttering stem to stern in their full glory in the frozen wind. New York Mayor John Hyland and other prominent dignitaries approached on the steamer *Highlander*, along with a small fleet of yachts, tugs, and launches in their wake. Their purpose is to welcome home the first American contingent of Yankees from the Great War. Often overlooked was the logistics of transporting all those soldiers and supplies from America to England. America did not have the necessary ships—England did. It was a sight to behold. Nothing proclaims war is over more succinctly than returning fighting men home.

Join me on board the *Mauretania* for the event. The khaki-clad doughboys (actually, we were conveying several aero squadrons and wounded casuals) were on deck singing "Oh You America." The four days of howling storms and huge waves had little effect on their voices. The mayor's fleet circled the ship, conveying their greetings with megaphones and various wireless devices—utterly ineffective unless the men paused to catch their collective breath. Police launches had their searchlights sweeping the decks. The men shouted to the circling boats, "When do we eat?" and, of most concern, "Has this state gone dry yet?" The chorus of their voices was a far cry from the singing of English comedian Harry lauder, who graciously performed on the way across.

At first, they were not allowed on the ship. The captain relented, and soon, the gangplank was lowered, and the mayor and his entourage scrambled aboard. Knights of Columbus secretaries passed out postage-stamp cards bearing the words "I am safe and sound" for the returning veterans to address to family and loved ones. The returning warriors sporadically sang "Oh How Dry We Are" in constant refrain, which was a lyric from Irving Berlin's latest song. I could not assess why that was of such great importance, the jolly Dr. Sydney Jones was thinking of other types of homecoming charity.

I left our book in the ship's library, along with hundreds of other books, in those beautifully crafted mahogany cabinets. None of the thousands of soldiers, passengers, or crew perusing the ship's library must have ever taken but a glancing curiosity of its contents. Perchance the title aroused no enthusiasm. When my beloved *Maury* was sent to the scrappers in 1935, our lost record must have been boxed along with all the other books from the shelves and sold in the auction. At least it was not burned as an offering to a deity, or you would not be reading these god-awful chronicles.

Dr. B S Jones' observation; a woman never wore the same hat twice on a cruise. All those women with all those wide-brimmed hats, always at risk to the gusting winds, rarely did one ever get swept overboard. How did they manage that?

One more story before my time wanes to vague. A patient under my care for a short time intrigued me. Physicians do get people who ignore their best therapy. A man will persevere in the face of medical conditions adamant in his destruction. One such person was American golf star Jesse Sweetser. In Saint Louis his name was Schweitzer, but a few German Americans altered their names because of the negative reaction in post war America.

The golfer married Agnes Lewis in February 1926, a comely Canadian girl, after a short two-week romance that began on the Lambton Golf Links in Toronto. He had won the National Intercollegiate in 1920, the American Amateur Championship in 1922, and the Metropolitan Amateur in 1925, yet the young Jesse rarely practiced nor took the game seriously, considering golf a minor sport. It was Agnes who persisted until he agreed to leave his New York stockbroking job to compete in England for the British Amateur in 1926. I hoped he thanked her for both.

While on the *Aquitania* in June 1926, I was entrusted with his care on his return to America after his being diagnosed with bronchitis, grip, and influenza after winning the British Amateur Championship. He was extremely exhausted when he boarded ship for the trip over to England, suffering several throat hemorrhages on that crossing, yet he played regardless of my consul. During a practice round at Muirfield, he collapsed and was carried from the links. Through sheer determination and courage, he played on to victory, but at a cost. My fellow British doctors acquiesced to his wishes and permitted him to sail home, injecting him with heroin, and more to inject if he relapsed.

On the return trip he was under my constant supervision, being so ill that he was not allowed on deck. I was relieved of that duty in New York Harbor when a coast guard cutter removed him to be rushed to a hospital. Afterward he went to a TB clinic in Asheville, North Carolina, his doctors fearing the worst. He took a year's rest and returned to business and semi-competitive golf for many more years. Hope you enjoyed that story. He was one tough customer.

Dr B Sydney Jones, Senior Medical Officer of the Cunard Fleet
says the language of the sea is in fact disappearing.
The sailors no longer talk of going "aft" of "forward"
but say they are going "front" or to the "end" of the ship.
And there is no "starboard" or "port" but "right" and "left"
and "above" and "below" have given place to "upstairs" or "downstairs."

—*Brooklyn Daily Eagle*, 2 August 1927

Beavington—the *B* in B. Sydney Jones stands for Beavington. My using the first letter only should be self-explanatory. I was born in 1866 in Surrey, England. My father, a Sydney also, was a doctor, taught medicine, and had a prosperous practice. Students were constantly in our home to be trained in the profession. Coexisting with my father on our small island would have been challenging, he was an accomplished senior surgeon at London's Saint Thomas's Hospital and sought-after lecturer. I had a mother, Mary, and a sister, Ethel. We had five servants—privileged, you might say. In 1893, the Royal College of Surgeons was kind enough to honor me with a degree and a medical license. Three years later, for youthful reasons deemed so important to me at that time, I went to sea. It would be thirty-six years before I would call my beloved island home again.

The war years found me at sea on cruisers and on land at the Chatham Naval Hospital. The British government awarded medals for war service to officers and men who risked being attacked while hostilities existed. Not sure I earned mine, but I did receive a Mercantile Marine War Medal and British War Medal. They did look very dignified on my uniform. In the midst of those years, I was appointed chief medical officer of the Cunard fleet, but you already knew I was the BIG CHIEF!

You might think all those years at sea deprived me of a conventional life, but a rather fortuitous event happened in 1926. I married my childhood sweetheart, Frances M. Sampson, a fine Englishwoman and perfect companion for this wave-weary alchemist. One thing I have learned is that there are no wrinkles upon the heart, and I have examined many beyond measure. The union included two grandchildren, to whom I now am teaching the Heathen rituals.

A reporter asked me what I should do when I had to give up the sea. "Private practice in England or maybe Italy," I responded. I did not make it to Italy. The captain and officers of the *Aquitania* presented me with a silver salver and silver tea service at the bittersweet conclusion of my final voyage. The tarnish is starless black now.

> A hundred years went by and what was left
> of this haughty and proud people full of
> free passions? They and all their generations
> had passed away.
>
> Pushkin

Judge our apparitions kindly. The Big Chief asks you to pardon the Heathen tribe's trespass into your time. I hope we were not a *mal de mer* for your twenty-first century's indifference. You are aware that I have a most wonderful potion for that ancient malady, and much less expensive than Red Raven Splits! A century ago many of our names would have been part and parcel of daily conversations. Previously, we had found ourselves banished from memory, a physical death not being sufficient. With artful contrivance, the goddess Themis, unveiling a whimsical smile, called us forth, for a parcel of reparation. To quote Haddon Chambers, "the long arm of coincidence" must have been at work for our temporary resurrection.

Greedily, we stole everything from that which briefly belonged to us—it was ours for the taking. Who condemns our excess? Nature intended genesis to be an adamant apostle of the succeeding generations claim by the demise of the foregoing. One glimpse of a child and you recognize it as inescapable, a second gaze allows your worldly weary soul to rejoice with all that has been created.

One day, all those life-giving seconds stopped with no apology. Trifle not a solitary tear for possibilities adrift, shed a torrent for entirety relinquished, cascading into the mighty deep, never to rise again. Passionately relish your own trice more.

Weaving through the forgotten mists of time long since exhausted, I hear a faint melancholic melody resonating from the strings of Mr. Hartley's violin. The gentle notes of the song "Traumerei" summon my return. The spell broken . . . Rejoin the tribe I must . . . My Heathen companions await.

> In the time yet to come, gather your senses when the blue moon gleams fearless and Aeolus breathes the winds gentle. You just may hear the mirthful sounds of mischievous phantoms hoisting a champagne glass proclaiming, "Oom Cum Pivvy Sinkit!"

MEDICAL EPILOGUE

ABOARD THE *LUCANIA* in 1906, Canadian MP Colonel James Domville had broken a leg. He had tripped in a companionway heading to supper in the saloon. The colonel was returning from England after raising three million dollars for an electric railroad in Canada. At the time, I believed internal operations are best executed over dry land, if possible, and delicate procedures should not be done on rolling seas. One cannot know when emergencies will arise, but no doctor feels inclined to be cutting into a breathing body on a moving ship bouncing along in waves large or small, at speed or not.

It is a tranquil September evening in 1921. Imagine yourself in the operatory on board one of the great ocean liners of my era, efficient, utilitarian, clean, and well provisioned. The surgical light brightly illumes our stricken patient. Two Heathen doctors, prepped for an operation, fixed their eyes upon Robert Mayer, saloon steward on the *Aquitania*, who has just received a healthy dose of ether. Commander Bainbridge, presently USN surgeon on the staff of Admiral Sims, is here to assist. The revenant of Dr. Reginald Fitz, the published authority on that perpetually offending organ, may have hovered overhead.

The newspaper article stated I was a specialist in abdominal surgery. That certainly placed the burden on the Big Chief. This day my skills will not be tested to the limit, and the seas are graciously calm. I make the first incision in the abdomen above—you guessed it—the area where the appendix resides. Mousie and Big Chief, assisted by Reginald's ghostly guidance, were successful.

That fiendish organ never tires of bothering me. During a westerly gale in February 1922, a seven-year-old boy named Robert Webster was overcome by an acute appendicitis. Immediate surgery was required, and assisted by Dr. Rossiter, the outcome was favorable. The seas were unwavering in their intensity throughout the procedure.

Three years later, a persistent two-day December storm was battering the *Aquitania*. Fifty windows were smashed. Five cabins and the promenade deck were flooded but, with consideration, not the operatory. One of our own crew, ship's dispenser William Odder, needed his appendix removed. Thrashing forty-foot waves showed no respect towards my patient, nor did they prevent me from operating. Life or death makes the decision for you. By now, one would think, I was becoming accustomed to surgery in rolling seas. Dr. Robert Blom was kind enough to assist me, a passenger pressed into service at the last minute.

By happy chance, some doctors deliver babies, I was glorified with the human appendix, Gordon Bennett. The patient survived. In medical school, the emphasis was not focused on that singular lump, or perhaps I nodded off through that lecture. I claim the distinction of having removed more of those damnable organs at sea than any physician whoever roamed an ocean. Since donors were few and sacrifices crucial for the most sacred Heathen rituals, I found the extraordinary skill of our chef had not diminished in his implementation of my special requests.

Dr. Bevington Sydney Jones leaves you with his *appendix.*
In it, you will find other Heathens who traveled with me
across the Atlantic. They are listed in the archive
although never signed, they remain Heathens nevertheless.

508. Alice Bourne Norton
509. Algeron St. John Brennan
510. Alice Osbourn
511. Lillian Russell
512. Lillian Hennesey
513. Maggie Ashton
514. Percy T. Morgan
515. Eugene de Sabla
516. James Lane
517. Ida Rene
518. James Emerson
519. Willard Bartlett
520. Miss E. H. MacDonald
521. Jack Herbert Parsons
522. Elsie Forbes

Honorary appointee

523. Kenneth H. Shaw, author

The Heathen Chronology

Founders, 17 September 1908

Constance Collier/ High Priestess

Alice Lloyd\/ Little Mother

Hugh Bellas

Tom McNaughto/, Phunny Phunster

D. M. G. Newton

Dr. B. Sydney Jone/, Big Chief

Arthur L. Pearse/ Little Chief

1 November 1910

Constance Collier

Freyda Harrision/ Red Mullet

Wm. Bainbridge/ Mousie

Fulton McMahon

Shirely Lloyd/ Shirely

Joseph Corbett/ Cupid Cherub

Leon Garcey

Robert Watchorn

Countess Von Ostheim

May Blayney

Dr. B. Sydney Jones

4 February 1911

Lallie Thurgate Williams

William H. Hossack/ Bro Billy

Lena Ashwell/ Queenie

Salvatore D. Antoni,/Salvation Muely

J. A. Corbett

Ion Hamilton Benn/ Big Benn

B. Sydney Jones

3 December 1910

Ellen Pauline Nathan Chase

Jessie Hale

Cedric Chivers

J. Frank Nicholson

20 December 1910

Irina Nyburgh/ Vivo

Alexander M Carlisle/ AM

Arthur Ernest Hills/ Arthurian Legs

Peter Walker/ Saltpeter

William Ragg Holt/ Scribendum

Edith Carlisle/ Pera

Harriet Blanche Lawrence\/ Bright Eyes

George H Doran, Dad

Albert Lund

25 February 1911

B. Sydney Jones

Suzanne Jackson/ Ruby

James A. Pitts/ Mormon Gayle

J. Adamson Parkyn

Duchess d'Olivaries/ Sister Duchess

Eric McKay Reid

Doris Field/ Christiana

Helen Kaufman/ Sister

7 May 1911

Dr. B. S. Jones

Mary Letche/, Sister Mary

Irene Fenwick/ Frizzie

Ernest Kent

Alexander Howard

S. D. Antoni/ Salvation Muely

18 May 1911

Amy Hoblyn

Muriel Barneson

Frank Roberts

Robert Deford

28 May 1911

Dr. Jones

Ida Barnard/ Eve

Pablo Escandon/ Gov

Myra Seymour,/ Mother

William Holmes Hossack

14, 15, 16 June 1911

Alice Lloyd

Robert B. Smith/ Jeff

Mark Leuscher/ Mutt Jr

Hazel Troutman/ Sister Trouty

A Popple/ Poppy

Alexander Howard

Bessie McNaughton/ Sister Betty

Elalia Grey/ Antipon

Chauncy McCormick/ Lodger

Tom McNaughton
Ernest Kent/ Garden
Emily Birmingham/ Sister Birmy

17 November 1911
George Doran/ Dad
Mary Noble Doran/ Sister Little
Leonard Peskett/ Kiltie
Dr. Jones

2 September 1911
Alice Lloyd
Alice McNaughton/ Flapper

13 September 1911
Dr. Jones
Donald Newton
Joseph W Stern/ the Little Lost Child
Leona Stern/ Sister Sterny
Morris Voss/ Brother Updike

23 September 1911
Dr. Jones
Ida Barnard
David D McIntyre/ Clan

25 September 1911
B. S. Jones
Ida Barnard
George Washington Clarke
Charles Butson
Henry Sanford

27 September 1911
Dr. Jones
Ida Barnrad/ Eve
Mary Galloway/ Comfort
Ernest Craig/ Kitten
Lee Ewart/ Saucy Kipper
John Keppie/ Neves Wind

24 October 1911
B. Sydney Jones
Arthur Pearse/ Little Chief
Fred Harrison/ Red Mullet
William Seamen Bainbridge/ Mousie

25 October 1911
Dr. B. Sydney Jones
Arthur Pearse
Katie Englis
Jessie Baskerville

Katie Inglis/ Mint Frappe
Jessie Baskerville,/ Bon Bon
Edgar Four/, Sandow

Edgar Fourt
Dr. Bainbridge
June Wheeler Bainbridge/ Octo
J. W. Williams/ Tempo
Ernest Nash/ Pacifico

17 November 1911
Herbert Roberts
Mrs. H. P. Roberts
Augusta Leach
Barbara MacRenzie
Charles Haddon Chambers
Kathryn Primley

17 March 1912
Letiha Barba
John MacNeill
W. P. Barba
William McCullen
Joseph Woods

26 March 1912
Dr. Sydney Jones
Wish Wynne/ Pepsin Hosey
Selwyn Goldstein/ Where?
Jean M Crippen\/ Doctor
Augusta Leech
William P. Leech

7 April 1912
Dr. Jones
David Watson Dyer/ Maine
Ida E. Williams/ Panky
James McCubbin/ Mac
Harold Nevanas/ the Mariner

26 May 1912
Dr. Jones
George Arliss/ Dizzy
Florence Arliss/ Bols
Arthur Smythe/ Boy

5 July 1912
Dr. Jones
Esme Hyde/ Lollipop
Florence Marshall/ Pettie
Mary Kingdon/ Box
Jacob Cahan/ Frugal
Walter Hyde/ Wodgie
J. Mario Korbel/ Sculpus

15 August 1912

Ernest Craig

Dr. Jones

Anna E Craig/ Flora

Anna Ernestine Craig/ Arizona

Angeline Holman/ Paw

Charles Holman/Lallapaloosa

John McGlie/ Maggie

18 October 1912

Dr. Jones

Philip Michael Faraday

Violet Maud Tree

21 November 1912

Dr. Jones

Juliette Martin/ Lackme

Anna Taylor/ Kennsy

George Elliot Fowler/ Chicken

Susanne Jackson/ Ruby

1 December 1912

Mabel F. Skarrat

Arthur M. Lawrence

Sidney Lister

12 December 1912

Dr. Jones

Patricia Collinge/ Ah Nooso

Ernst Craig

Alice Pauline Broxholm/ Fluffy

Frederick Cyril Broxholm/ Tom

21 December 1912

Dr. Jones

Herbert Beerbohm Tree

Herbert Kaufman

25 January 1913

Dr. Jones

Ethelwyn Leveaux/ Sister Sue/ PokeyNose

Winifred Faber/ Sister Peggy

Kurt Waldenstrom/

9 March 1913

Dr. Jones

Ernestine Craig Smith

Clarence Graff/ Gambit

5 June 1913

George Vits

Olive Powell Vits

6 June 1913

Mercy Cadwallader

Esther Gartley

Dr. Jones

W H Gartley
Helen Gartley
Albert Chandler/Dearie

15 June 1913
Alice Lloyd
Tom McNaughton
B Sydney Jones
Harriet Silverman/ Karnols
Alice McNaughton/ Flapper
Milton Aborn (P)
Irving Berlin/ Musical Pivvy
Sydne Silveman/ Skigie
J M Kelly/ Victoria
Clifford Hess/ Soft Pedal Pivvy
Bessie Hyams/ Kiddy
Franklin Wheaton Smith/ Pick Ax

3 October 1913
Dai Turgeon/ Sister Sunny
William Boosey/ Brother Bill

11 September 1913
Dr. Jones
Edgar Fourt/ Sandow
Maude Denison/ Sister Bunny
Leon J Garcey/ Brother Full Moon
Baron Hochwachter/ Brother Iggy

23 March 1914
Paul Friedman
Elsa Friedman
Julie Opp Faversham

30 May 1914
Margaret Mayo Selwyn/Sister Baby Mine
Leonore Harris/ Sister Patsy
Edgar Selwyn/ Brother Nasty Terrier
Leslie Fabe/ Black Cora

31 May 1914
Eva Kern/Sister Blondie

Francis Palmer/ Sister Bisquit
Roland N Moore/ Brother Terps

Jerome Kern/ Brother Laughing Husband

H Nye Chart/ Look Out

C Norman Coupland/ Brother Jam Pot

Holbrok Blinn/ Any Old Night
LSD
Dr. Jones
Arthur Pearse
Ruth Benson/ Official Terraplin

18 June 1914
Dr. Jones
Sister Liz
Kathryn Tyndall/ Sister Beauty
Alice Gale/ Sister 55

2 September 1914
Dr. Jones
Anna Taylor
Mayme McKenna/ Bunk
Thomas Hope Simpson/ Copper
Henry Earle/ Bubbles

16 September 1914
Dr. Jones
Rosalie Selfridge/ Sister Yum Yum
Violette Selfridge/ Sister Little
Katherine Stuart Burns/ Ki Ki
Gerald Browne/ Whiskey Bear

The Heathens bid you adieu.

WE EXISTED, ONLY not to you, until now. Come aboard for an unexpected experience in the first quarter of the previous century, when majestic steamships sheared the Atlantic waves before the Great War. Famous men Irving Berlin, Jerome Kern, Leo Carrillo, Sir Ion Benn, and George Arliss were members of a secret society on the RMS *Mauretania*. Actresses Constance Collier, Lena Ashwell, Alice Lloyd, Pauline Chase, Irene Fenwick, and Princess Paola of Saxe-Weimar were initiated. Mercy Cadwallader, the influential spiritualist, and Ethelwyn Leveaux, author Somerset Maugham's lover and painter Sir Gerald Kelly's muse, signed the sacred tome. Leonard Peskett, the *Mauretania*'s architect, and Alexander Carlisle, architect of the *Titanic*, joined the illustrious ranks. Their revival lies within these true stories of the 169 persons who were honor-bound to this tribe of Atlantic travelers. Become privy to the never-before-published secret rituals of the Select and Ancient Order of the Heathens. The HIGH PRIESTESS anticipated your arrival.